BASIC TRAINING COURSE

HOW TO DEAL WITH LIFE'S PITFALLS, PAINS, AND PROBLEMS

Nicolas Ellen, PhD

ECTC

Expository Counseling Training Center

Houston, Texas

Book Cataloging Data

Ellen, Nicolas André
How to Deal with Life's Pitfalls, Pains, and Problems
Includes bibliographical references
ISBN 978-1-952902-04-8 (pbk.)
ISBN 978-1-952902-05-5 (eBook)
1. Counseling 2. Christian Counseling 3. Christianity 4. Discipleship

Unless otherwise noted, scripture references taken from the
New American Standard Bible® (NASB),
Copyright © 1960, 1962, 1963, 1968, 1971, 1972, 1973, 1975, 1977, 1995 by
The Lockman Foundation.
Used by permission.
www.Lockman.org

Tree art on pages 18 and 22 adapted from an image © Can Stock Photo / aleksander1

Published by Expository Counseling Training Center
Houston, Texas
https://MyCounselingCorner.com

Contents

CONTENTS

Section 10
Decision-Making in the Will of God

Section 11
Living by Purpose

Section 12
The Cycle of Relationships

Section 13
Abuse, Separation / Divorce, Remarriage

Section 14
Understanding Sorrow / A Biblical View of Illness, Psychotropic Drugs, and Biblical Counseling

Bibliography

Pride / Humility

Understanding Pride

Key Point: Pride is at the root of every sin we commit and at the core of the problems we have with people and circumstances. Therefore, we need to understand the nature of pride if we are going to deal properly with the problems we face with people and circumstances.

I. The *Principle* of **Pride**: Pride is a mind set on *self* with resistance and/or a lack of submission to the will of God (Rom. 8:5-7).

   A. A mind governed by one's own assessment of self with resistance and/or a lack of submission to the will of God (Luke 18:9-14).

   B. A mind governed by one's own belief system about God, life, and people with resistance and/or a lack of submission to the will of God (Prov. 28:26).

   C. A mind governed by trust, confidence, or dependence in one's own abilities, accomplishments, academics, affluence, associations, or position in life, with resistance and/or a lack of submission to the will of God (Dan. 4:30-37).

   D. A mind governed by service of self, sustaining of self, satisfaction of self, or exalting one's self with resistance and/or a lack of submission to the will of God (Gen. 11:1-9).

II. The *Problem* of Pride: Pride is *detestable* to God and brings *detriment* to you from God when you walk in it (Prov. 6:16-17, Ps. 119:21).

    A. Pride is hated by God (Prov. 6:16-17).

    B. Pride puts you in opposition to God (Jas. 4:6).

    C. Pride leads God to bring destruction to your home (Prov. 15:25a).

    D. Pride leads to God's judgment of you (Prov. 16:5).

III. The *Practice* of Pride: Life is lived in being *consumed* with pleasing, providing for, or promoting of one's self with a lack of love for God and others (2 Tim. 3:1-4).

    A. Pride is revealed in being preoccupied with having one's way and using people to get it, resulting in confusion, disorder, and every evil thing in one's life (Jas. 3:13-16).

    B. Pride is revealed in one having a sense of entitlement to God's comfort, while getting angry when God allows discomfort in one's life (Jonah 4:5-9).

    C. Pride is revealed in one talking in a manner that reveals thinking too highly of oneself (Ps. 94:4).

    D. Pride is revealed in rebellion and/or disrespect of God and God-given authority in one's life (Neh. 9:1-26).

IV. The *Product* of Pride: Pride leads to a *disconnect* from God, a downfall in your life, and division with others (Hos. 7:10; Prov. 18:12, 29:23, 13:10).

    A. Pride hinders you from seeking the Lord (Hos. 7:10).

    B. Pride leads you to be deceived about who you really are (Jer. 49:16).

    C. Pride hinders you from genuine improvement (Prov 26:12).

    D. Pride brings shame to your life (Prov. 11:2).

E. Pride leads you to self-destruction (Prov. 16:18).

F. Pride leads you to stir up strife with others (Prov. 28:25).

V. The *Picture* of Pride: Pride will *manifest* itself in many ways and in various forms:

A. Arrogance—to exaggerate your own worth/importance.

B. Presumption—to suppose that something is true without checking because you think you know.

C. Unbelief—being skeptical of truth presented by God.

D. Self-Protection—keeping yourself from people, places, and things that may hurt you or disappoint you and using that as an excuse not to love.

E. Lack of forgiveness—holding a grudge against someone, not setting them free from the wrong they have committed against you even though they have sought your forgiveness.

F. Unbiblical control—seeking to regulate what people think, say, and do according to your personal standards and agenda and not God's will.

G. Self-preoccupation—preoccupation with what happens to you, through you, and for you.

H. Blame shifting—blaming your sin on the negligence of someone else or circumstances perceived as beyond your control.

I. Grumbling—being ungrateful in your situation or with people, believing you deserve better or more.

J. Lazy—doing things when you get ready or when you feel like it, not when God has commanded.

K. Self-sufficient—living and believing the lie that you do not need anyone and that you can handle life by yourself.

L. Unteachable—being unwilling to listen to instruction.

M. Lack of submission—being unwilling to follow instruction.

N. Perfectionism—setting standards that God did not set and seeking to live by them without any failure in them.

O. Pity party—always focusing on how bad you are and how bad you fail and feeling sorry for yourself as a result.

P. Resisting accountability—being unwilling to answer to people and be open to people who can help keep you from the people, places, products, or perspectives that lead you into sin or who can help you to confess, repent, and replace sin with right living.

Q. Defensiveness—seeking to escape or avoid criticism through some rationalization, justification, or denial.

I appreciate Stuart Scott's insights into the three topics of the "Picture of Pride, Process to Put Away Pride, and the Prize of Humility" from his booklet *From Pride to Humility.*

VI. The *Process* to Put Away Pride (Prov. 28:13-14)

A. Examine yourself (Prov. 14:8).

1. What has God said to me that I cannot accept?

2. Who do I compare myself with?

    a. What standards of thinking, behaving, and living govern my life?

    b. Do I live by what I feel or what God says?

    c. In what areas of my life have I chosen not to submit to God?

B. Examine your relationships (Rom. 12:9-21).

1. How often do I confess my faults to a person I have offended?

2. How often do I confess my hurts to a person I have offended?

3. Is my anger toward my family, friends, co-workers, and church members pleasing to God or displeasing to God?

4. Am I critical of family, friends, co-workers, and church leaders who do not do things according to my standards?

5. Do I give according to my feelings or God's standards?

6. Do I love according to my standards or God's standards?

C. Examine your response to God-given authority (1 Peter 2:13-17).

1. Am I (if a wife) submitting to my husband according to my standards or God's standards?

2. Am I submitting to leaders on the job and at church according to my standards or God's standards?

3. Do I have a biblical reason not to submit?

D. How do we deal with it? (Prov. 28:13-14)

1. Identify key areas where you have pride:

 a. Family

 b. Friends

 c. Work

 d. Finances

 e. Reputation

 f. Entertainment

2. Ask yourself, "Am I willing to live under God's authority in this area of my life?"

3. Confess to God your sin of pride in this area.

4. Ask God to give you a desire and will to repent in this area.

5. Learn God's truth in this area and meditate on it consistently.

6. Do the hard work of training in God's truth through the help of the Holy Spirit and other believers.

7. Expect difficulty, hardships, and resistance from all angles.

8. Allow God's grace, time, and truth to strengthen you as you train through the difficulty, hardship, and resistance.

9. Find a set of people that will encourage you, keep you accountable, and work with you.

Understanding Humility

Key Point: Humility glorifies God, and leads to a life with stability, transformation, and edification of others. If we want this kind of life, we need to understand and live a life of humility.

I. The *Principle* of Humility: Humility is a mind set on *Christ* with submission to the will of God (Rom. 8:5-7; Gal. 2:20; 2 Cor. 5:8-9, 15; Gal. 5:6, 13).

A. One who is walking in humility is focused on the Person, Practice, Plan, and Precepts of Jesus Christ.

B. One who is walking in humility recognizes that one's life is no longer one's own but belongs to Jesus Christ.

C. One who is walking in humility has a life committed to obedience to God in all aspects of life.

D. One who is walking in humility has a life committed to loving others, which works out in servanthood toward others.

II. The *Perspective* of Humility: One who walks in humility has a right view of *self*, others, life, and God as granted by God to see these truths (Rom. 12:3).

A. One who is walking in humility sees the greatness of God and the smallness of oneself in comparison to God (Job 42:2-6).

B. One who is walking in humility sees one's own sinfulness and is willing to surrender to God for mercy (Luke 18:9-14).

C. One who is walking in humility has the right view of one's own resources and abilities granted by God (Rom. 12:3).

D. One who is walking in humility has an accurate understanding of one's own roles and responsibilities in life in relation to God and others (John 22:22-36).

III. The *Picture* of Humility: Humility will manifest itself in many ways and in many forms:

A. Willingness and action in following the instructions of God.

B. Willingness and action in submitting to God-ordained authority.

C. Willingness and action in serving others without looking for anything in return.

D. Willingness and action in listening to and acting upon the wise counsel of others.

E. Being faithful, available, and teachable in all aspects of life.

F. Considering the interests of others and acting upon this without looking for anything in return.

G. Accepting what God allows without grumbling or complaining about it.

H. Submitting to what God says without grumbling or complaining about it.

I. Not preoccupied with self and what others think of oneself but preoccupied with thoughts of God and how to serve others.

IV. The *Prize* of Humility: One who walks in humility can expect God's *kindness* and empowerment for sanctification and service. This can be seen in various ways (Jas. 4:6).

A. Humility can lead to salvation (Job 22:29).

B. Humility can lead to God's justice on your behalf (Ps. 25:9).

C. Humility can lead to God giving you understanding of His ways (Ps. 25:9).

D. Humility can lead to God-given wisdom (Prov. 11:2).

E. Humility can lead to God-given honor (Prov. 29:23).

F. Humility can lead to God's exaltation (Luke 18:14).

G. Humility can lead to God answering yes to your prayer request (2 Chron. 7:14).

H. Humility can lead to God satisfying your desires accordingly (Ps. 145:18-19).

I. Humility can lead to God providing you with inner strength (Ps. 10:17).

V. The *Process* to Humility

A. Examine *yourself*.

1. What sin has God exposed that I am repenting of right now?

2. In what areas of my life am I obeying God right now?

3. Have I been giving thanks for everything or have I been complaining about people/places/things/circumstances?

4. What is preoccupying my thinking (serving or being served)?

B. Examine your *relationships*.

1. How often do I confess my sin and seek forgiveness from people I have sinned against?

2. How often do I confess my hurts to people who have offended me?

3. How do I speak the truth in love to others?

4. Am I encouraging more and criticizing less?

5. Am I serving others consistently or as I feel like it?

6. Am I on the defense when others tell me I am wrong or have sinned?

7. Am I teachable or only able to teach?

8. Do I have a hard time accepting being wrong, or is it becoming easier to deal with?

C. Examine your response to *authority*.

1. How often do I (if a wife) follow the instructions of my husband?

2. How often do I follow the instructions of leaders on my job, at church, in the government?

3. Do I submit to leaders according to my standards or God's standards?

4. Do I have biblical reasons not to follow the instructions given by the authorities over me?

5. How often do I fight against instructions that I don't agree with or don't feel like doing?

6. Do people have to instruct me in a certain way before I submit, or do I submit as unto the Lord?

D. Commit to the put-off/put-on *process*.

1. Ask yourself: "Am I willing to live under God's authority in all areas of my life?"

2. Confess to God your sin of pride in the areas where you find pride.

3. Learn how God wants you to walk in those areas of your life by studying God's Word and seeking wise counsel.

4. Pray for God's wisdom on how to apply what He gives you to do.

5. Through the power of the Holy Spirit and support of other believers, set goals on a weekly basis for doing what God commanded.

6. Work daily at accomplishing these goals of obedience.

7. Expect difficulty and resistance from your flesh, the world, and the devil.

8. When you fall, get up and keep training in the truth.

9. Let others support you and hold you accountable.

God-Centered

Slave of God

Romans 6:22: But now having been freed from sin and enslaved to God, you derive your benefit, resulting in sanctification, and the outcome, eternal life.

Psalm 119:105: Your word is a lamp to my feet, and a light to my path.

We have two choices in life. We either choose to be God-centered or self-centered. The more we choose to be self-centered, the more we are held captive by our sin. The more we choose to be God-centered, we are freed from sin but walk in slavery to God, resulting in God's glory and our greatest good.

Self-Centered

Slave of Sin

Proverbs 5:22: His own iniquities will capture the wicked, and he will be held with the cords of his sin.

2 Timothy 3:1-4: But realize this, that in the last days difficult times will come. For men will be lovers of self, lovers of money, boastful, arrogant, revilers, disobedient to parents, ungrateful, unholy, unloving, irreconcilable, malicious gossips, without self-control, brutal, haters of good, treacherous, reckless, conceited, lovers of pleasure rather than lovers of God.

Point of Choice

Graphics based on an idea developed by Cathy Poulos.

I have appreciated the insights on this topic about "Idols of the Heart" by Mark Dutton.

The Point of Choice

Key Point: At the end of the day, a person only has two choices: to be self-centered or God-centered. This drives every other issue in life he or she encounters. The more we choose to be self-centered, the more we are held captive by our sin. The more we choose to be God-centered, we are freed from sin but walk in slavery to God, resulting in God's glory and our greatest good. The condition of our lives is determined by the choices we have made in life. Genuine biblical counseling helps individuals to understand this reality and to pursue the choice of being God-centered.

I. We Choose to Be God-Centered or Self-Centered (Gal. 5:16-25). *(See Illustration of Point I.)*

A. When we are God-centered, we choose to live our lives for God, resulting in doing things according to God's standards (Ps. 119:105).

B. When we are self-centered, we choose to live our lives for ourselves, resulting in doing things according to our own agenda (2 Tim. 3:1-4).

C. When we choose to live for ourselves instead of living for God, we will live in slavery to sin (Prov. 5:22).

D. When we choose to live for God instead of living for ourselves, we live in slavery to God (Rom. 6:22).

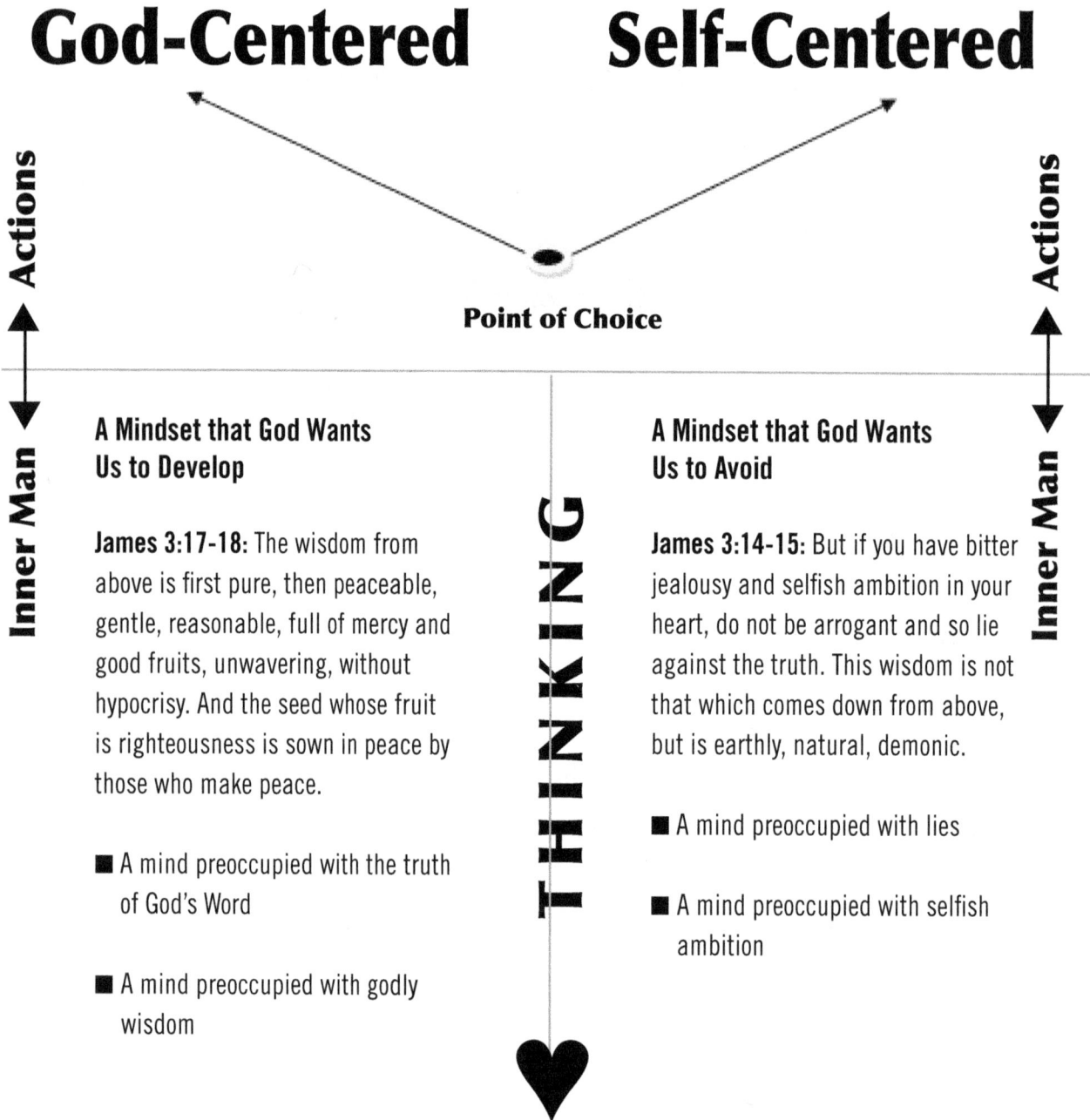

God-Centered   Self-Centered

Actions

Inner Man

Point of Choice

THINKING

A Mindset that God Wants Us to Develop

James 3:17-18: The wisdom from above is first pure, then peaceable, gentle, reasonable, full of mercy and good fruits, unwavering, without hypocrisy. And the seed whose fruit is righteousness is sown in peace by those who make peace.

■ A mind preoccupied with the truth of God's Word

■ A mind preoccupied with godly wisdom

A Mindset that God Wants Us to Avoid

James 3:14-15: But if you have bitter jealousy and selfish ambition in your heart, do not be arrogant and so lie against the truth. This wisdom is not that which comes down from above, but is earthly, natural, demonic.

■ A mind preoccupied with lies

■ A mind preoccupied with selfish ambition

Actions

Inner Man

II. Our choices are driven by our thoughts (Rom. 8:5). *(See illustration of Point II.)*

    A. When we are self-centered, our thoughts are dominated by lies and selfish ambition (Jas. 3:13-16).

    B. As a result of those lies and selfish ambition, our thoughts tend to be driven and reduced to what we have been denied, what we believe we deserve, what we want, what we think we should have, or what we think we need. We become friendly with the world and unfriendly with God (Jas. 4:1-10).

    C. When we are God-centered, our thoughts are dominated by truth and wisdom (Jas. 3:17-18).

    D. As a result of being dominated by truth and wisdom, our thoughts tend be driven by what God commands of us and how to live according to that. We focus on things such as what God promises to do for us and when to expect it. We tend also to focus on what God is doing for us and has done for us, as well as what we can be doing for others and how to do it approriately (Jas. 3:17-18).

God

Self

Drawing near to God • Kindness
Self-control • Faith • Goodness
Patience • Love • Peace of God
Self-sacrificing • Humility •
Gentleness • Merciful • Wisdom
Joy • Confidence before God

Selfishness • Sense of Guilt
Sarcasm • Demanding • Anger •
Rage • Arrogance • Deceit • Fear
of Judgment • Liar • Cruelty •
Divisiveness • Abuse • Manipulative
• Jealousy • Hatred • Immorality •
Fleeing when no one is chasing

Galatians 5:16, 22-26

Galatians 5:17-21

Actions

Inner Man

THINKING

Thoughts Motivated by the Holy Spirit

Desire to Know Jesus Christ

Thoughts Motivated by the Flesh (Indwelling Sin)

Hedonism–Preoccupation with whatever brings me pleasure apart from God

Desire to become like Jesus Christ	Appreciating the blessings of God; Anticipating the return of Jesus Christ	Desire to be useful to Jesus Christ	AUTONOMY Not having to answer to anyone	MATERIALISM Preoccupation with material things	ENTITLEMENT Believing I deserve whatever I want or pursue

Romans 8:5b: "but those who are according to the Spirit, [set their minds on] the things of the Spirit."

Romans 8:5a: "Those who are according to the flesh set their minds on things of the flesh"

III. Our thoughts are motivated by the flesh (sin in our hearts) or by the Holy Spirit (Rom. 8:1-14). *(See illustration of Point III.)*

A. When our thoughts are motivated by the flesh (sin in our hearts), we are preoccupied with issues such as hedonism (whatever brings me pleasure apart from God), autonomy (independence from authority; not having to answer to anyone), materialism (love of material things), and entitlement (believing I deserve whatever I want or pursue) to dominate our thinking.

B. This leads to further disobedience to God. We will see attitudes and actions such as anger, hatred, immorality, jealousy, abuse, cruelty, lying, selfish ambition, arrogance, rage, sarcasm, or selfishness. This leads to a guilty conscience, a fear of God's judgment, and a desire to escape God's judgment, which results in trying to flee from the inevitable consequences of disobedience to God (2 Tim. 3:1-9, Prov. 28:1).

C. When our thoughts are motivated by the Holy Spirit, we tend to be preoccupied with a desire to know Jesus Christ, to become like Jesus Christ, to be useful to Jesus Christ, the return of Jesus Christ, and the blessings in this life and the life to come from Jesus Christ our Lord.

D. This leads to further obedience to God. We will see attitudes and actions such as humility, patience, peace, joy, self-sacrifice, kindness, goodness, mercy, love, faith, gentleness, self-control, and wisdom. This leads to a peaceful conscience, a confidence in the presence of God, and a desire to draw near to God, which results in our drawing near to God (Gal. 5:22-25).

To Be

Appreciated Great

Loved Accepted Served

In Charge Happy Approved of

Understood Satisfied Significant

Comfortable Safe Respected

Held in High Regard

Viewed as Competent

To Have Influence

To Never Hurt Again

To Have Our Way

To Have Control

**Desires We Treasure and Worship Above
Loving God and Loving Others**

IV. When our thoughts are driven by the flesh (sin in our hearts) we will begin to worship our desires, turning them into the lusts of our lives (Jas. 4:1-3). *(See Illustration of Points IV and V)*

A. Our minds will be set on things below instead of things above, leading us to make self-interest a priority over God's will. We focus less and less on loving God and loving others; we focus more and more on using God and using others according to our self-interest (Phil. 3:17-19, Jas. 3:13-4:3).

B. Our desires will become preoccupations, resulting in our looking for avenues to satisfy these desires we have started to worship. We look to any person, place, product, or perspective we believe will satisfy these desires above loving God and loving others (Jas. 4:1-3).

C. We will build our lives around these desires we have started to worship above loving God and loving others (Phil. 3:17-19).

D. We will become servants of our flesh to satisfy these desires we have started to worship above loving God and loving others (Gal. 5:16-21).

V. As we make choices according to the desires we have begun to worship, we will find ourselves on a path of difficulty and hard times (Prov. 13:15). *(See Illustration of Points IV and V.)*

A. We will become a slave to that which we pursue above loving God and loving others (2 Peter 2:18-19).

B. We will develop sinful habits that are hard to repent of and replace as a result of pursuing those desires we worship above loving God and loving others (Prov. 5:21-22).

C. We will reap negative consequences of our sinful habits and pursuit of those desires we worship above loving God and loving others (Gal. 6:7-8).

D. We will have a negative effect on the lives of those around us as a result of pursuing those desires we worship above loving God and loving others (1 Cor. 5:1-6).

What Is the Situation?

What is happening? When? Where? With whom?

What do you want that you're not getting? What are you getting that you don't want?

Are you God-Centered or Self-Centered?

God-Centered

Self-Centered

8 What feelings are you displaying that reflect God-centeredness?

What words are you expressing that display God-centeredness?

What behaviors are you displaying that reveal God-centeredness?

What ways are you relating that display God-centeredness?

1 What feelings are you displaying that reflect self-centeredness?

What words are you expressing that display self-centeredness?

What behaviors are you displaying that reveal self-centeredness?

What ways are you relating that display self-centeredness?

7 What God-centered desires need to replace the self-centered desires?

THINKING

5 What God-centered thoughts need to replace the self-centered thoughts?

6 What God-centered motives need to replace the self-centered motives?

4 What are your self-centered desires?

THINKING

2 What are your self-centered thoughts?

3 What are your self-centered motives?

WALK IN THE SPIRIT →

← RECOGNIZE REPENT and REPLACE

Luke 9:23-25

1 John 1:9

Ephesians 4:17-24

Philippians 2:5

Colossians 3:5-7

Galatians 5:16, 22-23

VI. We must turn from a self-centered life to a God-centered life through the person, power, and precepts of Jesus Christ (Rom. 13:8-14). *(See Illustrations of Point VI.)*

A. We must identify the areas of our lives where we are dominated by lies, selfish ambition, hedonism, autonomy, materialism, entitlement, and lustful pursuits above loving God and loving others. We must identify where this is happening in our attitudes, intentions, desires, words, actions, relationship patterns, and service to God, and confess and repent of these things (Prov. 28:13-14).

B. We must decide to make God a priority in all that we think, say, and do (1 Cor. 10:31).

C. The areas of our lives where we are dominated by lies, selfish ambition, hedonism, autonomy, materialism, entitlement, and lustful pursuits must be replaced with specific obedience to God in those areas (Eph. 4:17-32, Col. 3:1-25).

D. In other words, we must guard our hearts from self-centeredness by walking in genuine love for God and love for others in our attitudes, intentions, desires, words, actions, relationship patterns, and service.

Discussion Questions

1. When looking at the choices that you have made today, were you self-centered or God-centered in your choices? Write down your findings.

_____

_____

_____

_____

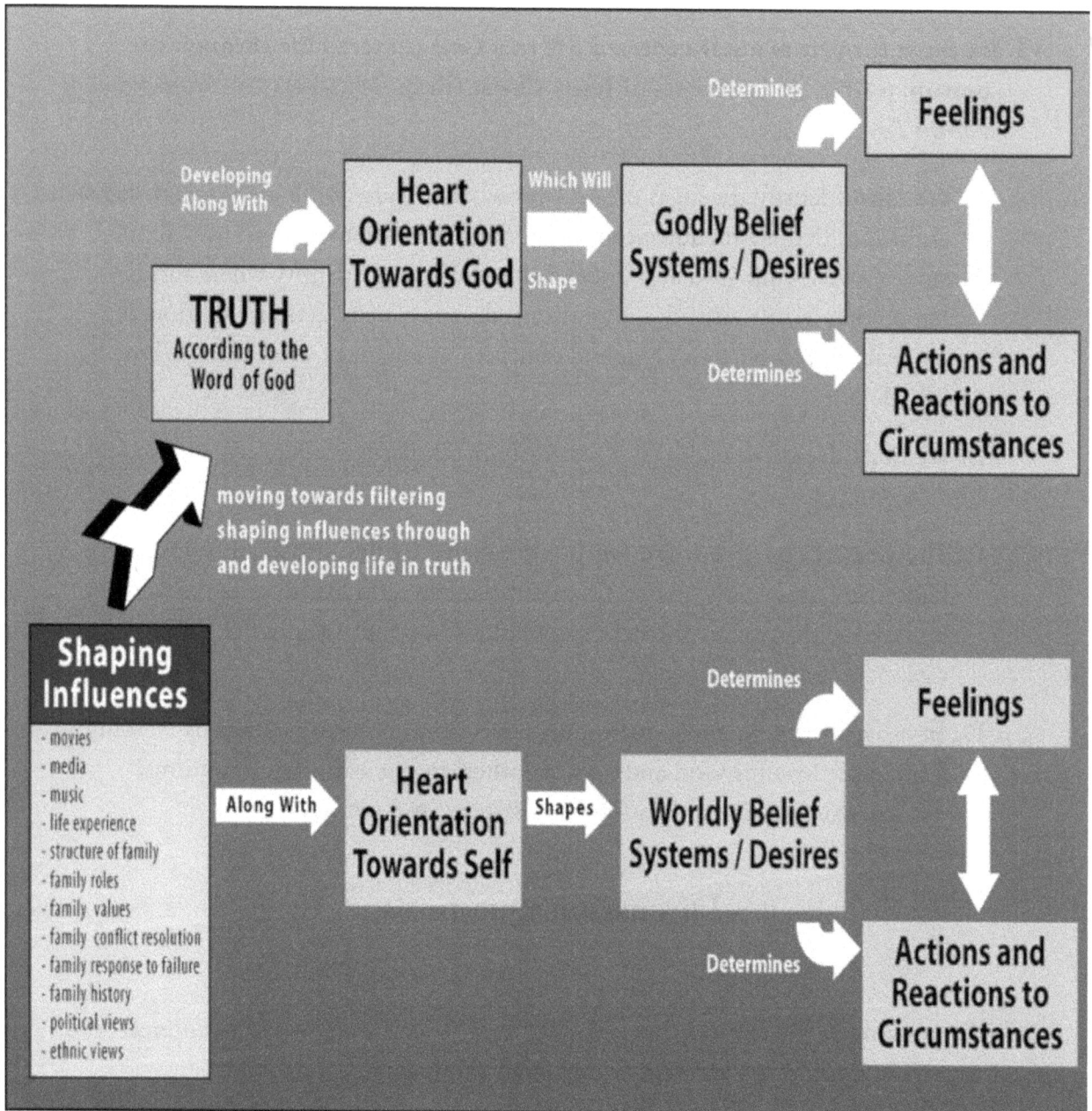

Feelings

Determines

Developing
Along With

Heart Orientation Towards God

Which Will

Godly Belief Systems / Desires

Shape

Determines

Actions and Reactions to Circumstances

TRUTH
According to the
Word of God

moving towards filtering
shaping influences through
and developing life in truth

Shaping Influences
- movies
- media
- music
- life experience
- structure of family
- family roles
- family values
- family conflict resolution
- family response to failure
- family history
- political views
- ethnic views

Along With

Heart Orientation Towards Self

Shapes

Worldly Belief Systems / Desires

Determines

Feelings

Determines

Actions and Reactions to Circumstances

Graphics by Adrian Baxter

2. Identify your thought patterns that are rooted in lies and selfish ambition, then identify your thought patterns that are rooted in truth and godly wisdom. Explain how these thought patterns determined your choices above.

_____

_____

_____

_____

3. What desires have you allowed to become a form of worship, resulting in further complications in your life?

_____

_____

_____

_____

4. What loving thoughts, motives, desires, words, actions, relationship patterns, and service do you need to walk in to replace your sin?

_____

_____

_____

_____

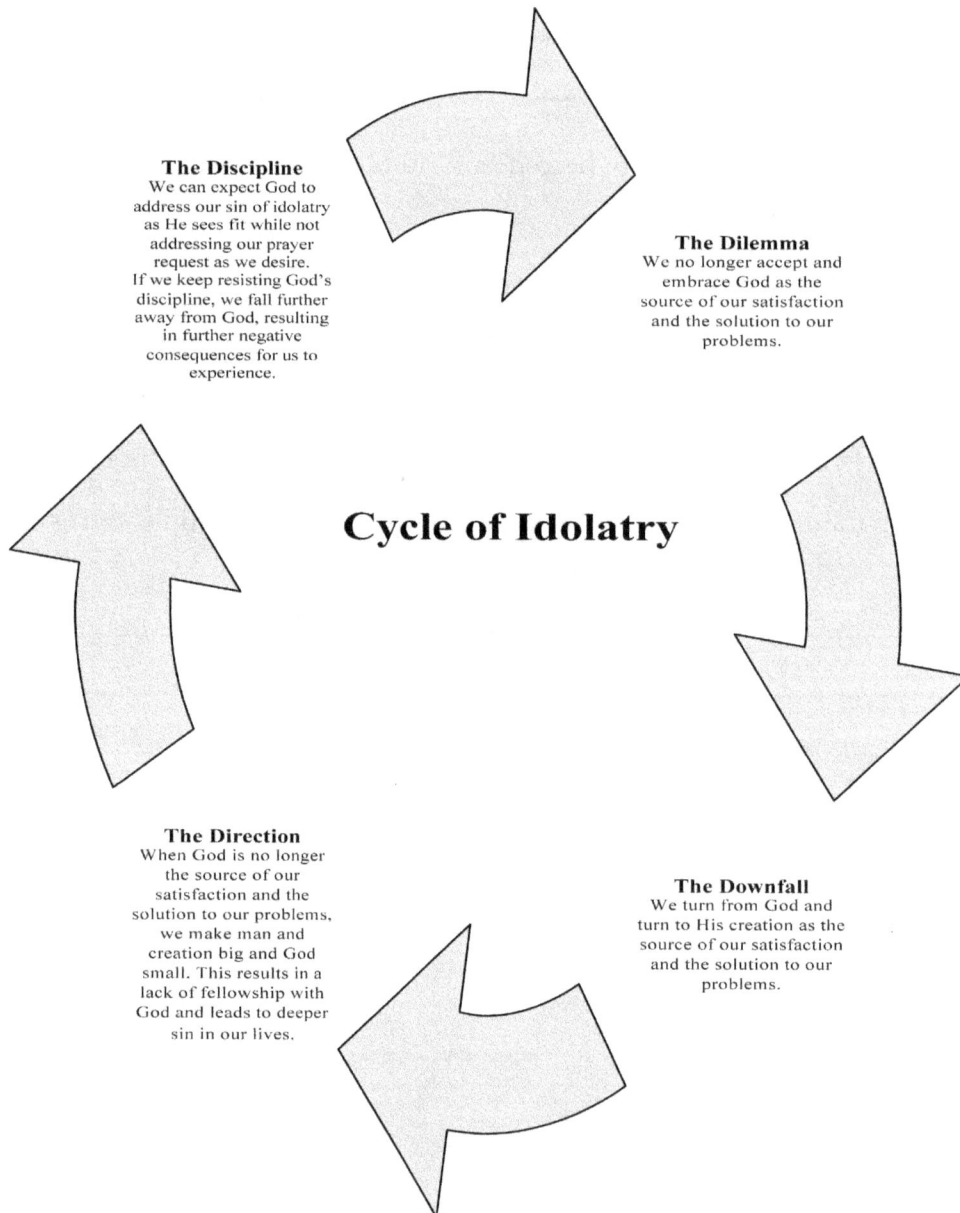

The Discipline
We can expect God to address our sin of idolatry as He sees fit while not addressing our prayer request as we desire. If we keep resisting God's discipline, we fall further away from God, resulting in further negative consequences for us to experience.

The Dilemma
We no longer accept and embrace God as the source of our satisfaction and the solution to our problems.

Cycle of Idolatry

The Direction
When God is no longer the source of our satisfaction and the solution to our problems, we make man and creation big and God small. This results in a lack of fellowship with God and leads to deeper sin in our lives.

The Downfall
We turn from God and turn to His creation as the source of our satisfaction and the solution to our problems.

3

Idolatrous Lust

Understanding Idolatry

I. The *Characteristics* of Idolatry (Jer. 2:13)

A. Idolatry is depending on some aspect of life or creation as you should depend on God, which in Jeremiah was categorized as broken cisterns. Broken cisterns are manmade and unreliable large pits dug in the rock, covered with plaster and used to gather rainwater. When cracks developed in the cisterns, they would hold no water—unlike the reliable natural springs of water that always provided water no matter the situation. This "living" water was used to symbolize God. (Dyer, *Bible Knowledge Commentary*)

B. Idolatry is dependence on some aspect of life or creation at the level of worship above God, in order to get what we treasure above God.

C. Idolatry is the dependence on certain aspects of life or creation at the level of worship above God, making them the avenues to our satisfaction and solutions to our problems.

D. Idolatry is the preoccupation with some aspect of life or creation above and apart from the Creator to satisfy some longing(s) of our hearts that have become the lusts of our hearts.

II. The *Creation* of Idolatry (Jer. 2:13)

A. Idols are created when we no longer look to God as the source of our satisfaction.

B. Idols are created when we no longer look to God as the solution to our problems.

C. When we no longer look to God as the source of our satisfaction, we look to His creation to bring it to us.

D. When we no longer to look to God as the solution to our problems, we look to His creation to bring it to us.

III. The *Criticism* and *Consequences* of Idolatry (Jer. 2:13, Ezek. 14:3)

A. Idolatry is evil in the sight of God.

B. Idolatry leads you away from serving God to serving His creation.

C. Idolatry leads you to stumble into further sin.

D. Idolatry leads God to address you according to your sin of idolatry instead of the request you bring to Him.

IV. The *Categories* of Idolatry

Remember that idolatry is the dependence on certain aspects of life or creation at the level of worship above God, making them the avenues of our satisfaction and solutions to our problems. Idolatry is the preoccupation with some aspect of life or creation above and apart from the Creator to satisfy some longing(s) of our hearts that have become the lusts of our hearts. *Idolatry* could be:

A. Depending on people

B. Depending on places

C. Depending on products

D. Depending on perspectives

E. Depending on positions

F. Depending on power

G. Depending on platforms of influence

H. Depending on politics

I. Depending on money

J. Depending on medication

K. Depending on media

L. Depending on ministry

Understanding Lust

I. The Characteristics of the Lusts of Our Hearts (Jas. 1:13-14)

A. Lusts of our hearts are longings that have become constant cravings of our hearts in an evil or wrong way.

B. Lusts of our hearts are longings that have moved from something we want to something we must have, making something that was once a good thing now an evil thing. This process makes it a sin in our lives because we are consumed with it above God and His will.

C. Lusts of our hearts are longings that have become such a preoccupation of our hearts that we are easily enticed by the devil when it comes to them, because they have become inordinate, sinful affections of our soul.

D. Lusts of our hearts are longings that have become such a preoccupation of our hearts that we are willing to sin to obtain them, sin to keep them, sin when do not receive them, or sin when we lose them. This makes those longings a worship in our lives above worship and obedience to God.

II. The Commitment to the Lusts of Our Hearts (Ezek. 33:31)

A. When we are committed to the lusts of our hearts, we will still listen to truth and delight in the truth we hear, but we will not obey that truth because we are preoccupied with the lusts of our hearts.

B. When we are committed to the lusts of our hearts, they become a constant topic of discussion.

C. When we are committed to the lusts of our hearts, we are in constant pursuit of obtaining them.

D. When we are committed to the lusts of our hearts, we do not find obedience to God something to be treasured above those lusts we have treasured in our hearts.

III. The Cancer of the Lusts of Our Hearts (Jas. 4:1-4)

A. The lusts of our hearts can lead us to kill others or at least be envious of them.

B. The lusts of our hearts can lead us to create conflict with others.

C. The lusts of our hearts can lead us to pray selfishly.

D. The lusts of our hearts can lead us to be friends with the world's system, resulting in our acting as enemies of God.

IV. The Consequences of the Lusts of Our Hearts (Jas. 1:15, Gal. 6:7-8)

A. The lusts of our hearts lead to walking in further sin in our thoughts, words, or actions.

B. Walking in further sin in our thoughts, words, or actions reveals that we are walking in the flesh, which leads to corruption in our lives and ultimately leads to death.

C. This could be physical death where, as a result of a Christian's unrepentant sin, he/she is now disciplined by God by being taken from earth to be with Him and losing rewards for eternity as a result of constant disobedience on earth (1 Cor. 11:23-32).

D. This could be eternal death where, as a result of an unbeliever's life of sin, he/she now faces the consequences of rejecting God and living a life of sin. That life ends in burning in hell forever (Rev. 20:11-15).

V. The Categories of the Lusts of Our Hearts

Remember, *lusts* of our hearts are desires we believe we cannot do without being satisfied. We are willing to sin to obtain them, sin to keep them, sin when we do not receive them, or sin when we lose them. Therefore, we make those longings a worship in our lives above worship and obedience to God. It could be a desire:

A. To be loved

B. To be accepted

C. To be understood

D. Never to be hurt or disappointed

E. To be respected

F. To be served

G. To have personal preferences accommodated at all times

H. To be viewed as competent

I. To be approved of

J. To belong to someone

K. To be held in high regard

L. To be significant to others

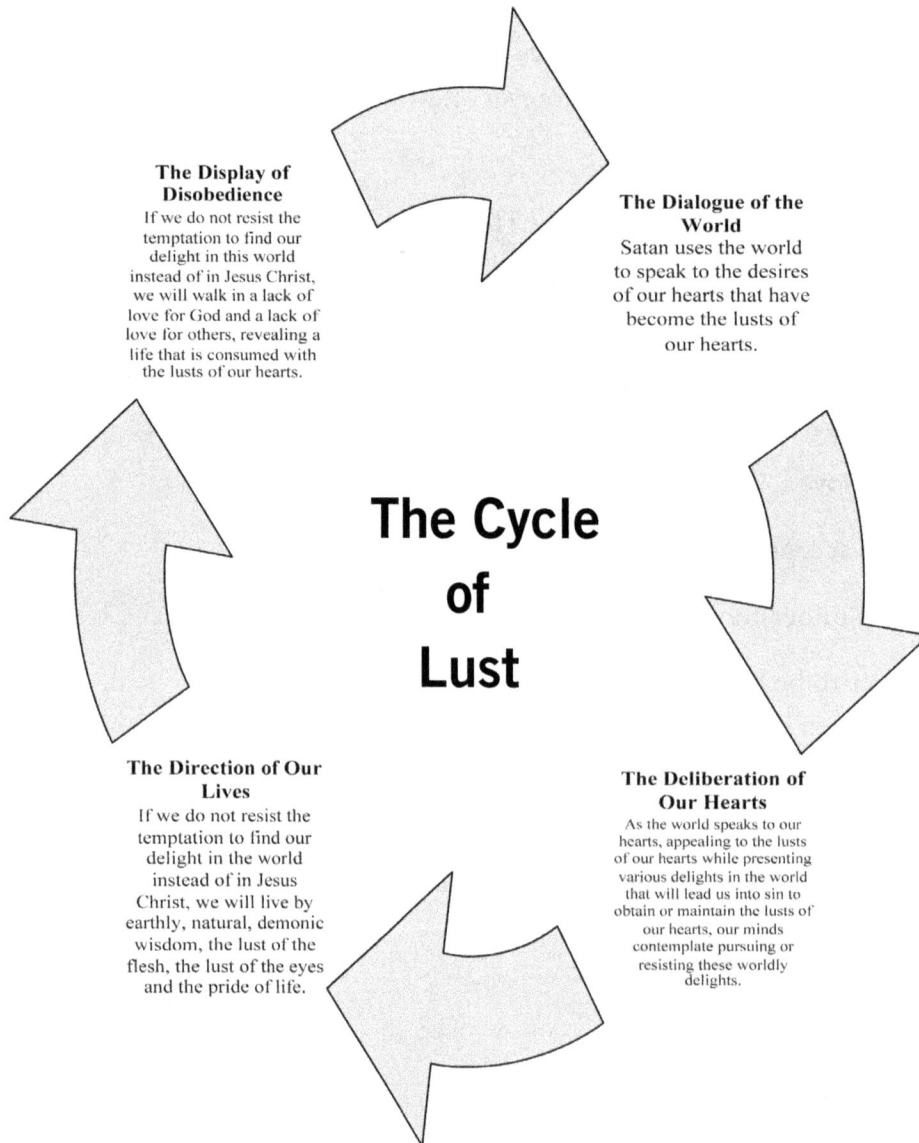

The Display of Disobedience
If we do not resist the temptation to find our delight in this world instead of in Jesus Christ, we will walk in a lack of love for God and a lack of love for others, revealing a life that is consumed with the lusts of our hearts.

The Dialogue of the World
Satan uses the world to speak to the desires of our hearts that have become the lusts of our hearts.

The Cycle of Lust

The Direction of Our Lives
If we do not resist the temptation to find our delight in the world instead of in Jesus Christ, we will live by earthly, natural, demonic wisdom, the lust of the flesh, the lust of the eyes and the pride of life.

The Deliberation of Our Hearts
As the world speaks to our hearts, appealing to the lusts of our hearts while presenting various delights in the world that will lead us into sin to obtain or maintain the lusts of our hearts, our minds contemplate pursuing or resisting these worldly delights.

M. To be satisfied by others

N. To maintain a favorable position with others

O. To be secure and safe

P. Never to be alone

Q. To have someone exposed for the way they have mistreated us

R. To have someone suffer the consequences for what they did to us

The Interaction of Idolatry and Lust

Definition of *Idolatrous Lust*: Something you bow down to that you believe will bring you what you truly treasure, while bowing down to what you truly treasure in place of the living God. It is the various aspects of life and creation we worship above the Creator, as well as the basic ways we worship the creation above the Creator (Rom. 1:18-32).

I. The *avenues* we pursue and bow down to in the form of worship (idols), along with these treasures we bow down to in the form of worship (lusts), make up the idolatrous lust in our lives (Rom. 1:18-25). Following are some examples of what we substitute for loving God and loving others.

A. Bowing down to *people* (*idol*) as we should to God to receive the *acceptance* we treasure and crave in an inordinate way (*lust*)

B. Bowing down to *education* (*idol*) as we should to God in order to be *viewed as competent*, which we treasure and crave in an inordinate way (*lust*)

C. Bowing down to *money* (*idol*) as we should to God to receive the *comfort* we treasure and crave in an inordinate way (*lust*)

D. Bowing down to *control* (*idol*) as we should to God to receive the *security* we treasure and crave in an inordinate way (*lust*)

II. We are led by a process into *idolatrous lust*:

A. *Mindset*: Your mind is set on things below instead of things above (Phil. 3:17-19).

B. *Motivation*: You begin to make self-interest a priority above God's will (Jas. 3:13-4:3).

C. *Meditation*: Your desires become preoccupations that evolve into lusts (Jas. 4:1-3).

D. *Methods*: You look for avenues to satisfy your desires that have now become lusts.

E. *Manner*: You bow down and submit to these avenues in order to obtain what you have turned into lusts, thus making them idols you bow down to in order to get what you lust after (Phil. 3:17-19).

F. *Mastered*: You become a servant of your flesh (Gal. 5:16-21).

III. How Do You Repent of Idolatrous Lusts? (Prov. 28:13-14)

A. Identify desires or cravings that have preoccupied your mind to the point of lust.

B. Identify the avenues you have pursued and thus have bowed down to in the place of God, in order to obtain these desires or cravings that have preoccupied your mind to the point of lust.

C. Identify the sinful thoughts, attitudes, and behaviors that have come about as a result of desires or cravings that have preoccupied your mind to the point of lust.

D. Confess to God and others the lusts, idols, sinful thoughts, sinful attitudes, and sinful behaviors you have identified.

E. Replace your lusts, idols, sinful thoughts, sinful attitudes, and sinful behaviors you have identified with genuine worship of God, godly thoughts, godly attitudes, and godly behaviors.

F. Decide to make God your priority over all and everything.

G. Guard your heart.

Examining the Heart Journal

1. What did you want today or what were you expecting to happen today?

_____

_____

_____

2. Who did you want it from or expect it to come from?

_____

_____

_____

3. What desire(s) would this fulfill in your life?

_____

_____

_____

4. How much of your time was spent thinking, speaking, and acting on what you wanted?

_____

_____

_____

5. What ways did you sin in thoughts, words, or actions to get what you wanted?

_____

_____

_____

6. What ways did you sin in thoughts, words, or actions when you did not get what you wanted?

_____

_____

_____

7. What person(s) did you sin against to get what you wanted?

_____

_____

_____

8. What person(s) did you sin against because you did not get what you wanted?

_____

_____

_____

9. What were your attitudes and actions like toward God and others as a result of getting what you wanted today?

_____

_____

_____

10. What were your attitudes and actions like toward God and others as a result of not getting what you wanted today?

_____

_____

_____

11. What biblical standards or principles could you use to explain your thoughts, words, and actions today?

_____

_____

_____

12. What biblical standards or principles should you have practiced in thoughts, words, or actions today?

_____

_____

_____

13. Were your thoughts, words, and actions toward others based primarily on how you felt or what God commanded? Explain.

_____

_____

_____

4

Understanding Worry

I. The *Content* of Worry (Ps. 139:23)

David asks God to reveal David's *anxious* thoughts. In the context of this passage, *anxious* means worried. To understand what God would reveal in David, we need to define *worry* in the context of what is very important to you from and in this present world.

   A. Disturbing or disquieting thoughts of the mind, due to preoccupation with the possibility of not getting something you want or need

   B. Disturbing or disquieting thoughts of the mind, due to preoccupation with the possibility of losing something you want or need

   C. Disturbing or disquieting thoughts of the mind, due to preoccupation with the possibility of getting something you do not want or need

   D. In essence, worry is the fear of not getting something you want or need, the fear of losing something you want or need, or the fear of getting something you don't want or need as a result of being consumed and controlled by the things that are very important to you from and in this world.

II. The *Cause* of Worry (Luke 10:38-42)

Jesus *challenged* Martha about her worry. Martha exposes to us what causes worry.

   A. Worry is caused by reducing life to what you want and what you think you need from and in this world, resulting in the fear of not getting something you want or need, the fear of losing something you want or need, or the fear of getting something you don't want or need from this world (intangible) and in this world (tangible).

B. Worry is caused by trying to control the good and bad that God controls in your life, instead of enjoying and enduring what God ordains in your life. This results in the fear of not getting something you want or need, the fear of losing something you want or need, or the fear of getting something you don't want or need from and in this world.

C. Worry is caused by trusting one's own knowledge or past experience and evaluating things according to that knowledge or past experience without considering or acting on God's Word. This results in the fear of not getting something you want or need, the fear of losing something you want or need, or the fear of getting something you don't want or need from and in this world.

D. In essence, worry is caused by one's interpretation of a situation apart from trusting God's sovereignty, sufficiency, or wisdom, which results in preoccupation with your own cares, riches, personal standards, or past experiences.

III. The *Characteristics* of Worry (Prov. 12:25)

Worry can create a heavy burden in one's *heart*. When something has become a heavy burden in your life, it *controls* and *consumes* you. Following are examples of how worry can result in loading your heart down with burdens.

A. Sometimes when you worry, you are controlled and consumed with the outcome of situations/circumstances.

B. Sometimes when you worry, you are controlled and consumed with the responses and reactions of people.

C. Sometimes when you worry, you are controlled and consumed with losing or gaining the needs or wants of life.

D. In essence, when you worry, you are controlled and consumed with things you can't keep from happening or things you can't cause to happen, resulting in your heart being loaded down with this burden. (This can lead to irresponsibility in the things you can control.)

IV. The *Counteractions* to Worry

A. Identify the fears that have consumed your time.

B. Identify the desires behind the fears (behind every fear there is a desire for something (e.g., fear of rejection = desire for approval).

C. Identify the people, places, things, and situations you believe are the source and the solution to your needs, desires, and problems.

D. Confess and repent of trying to control the uncontrollable (Job 38-42, Prov. 28:13-14).

E. Confess and repent of making people, places, and outcome of events the idols of your heart (Ezek. 14:1-11).

F. Confess and repent of making the desires of your heart lusts in your life (Jas. 1:13-14, 4:1-3).

G. Study, learn, and accept the sovereignty of God in all things (Eccles. 3:1-11, 7:13-14, 9:1, 11:5; Col. 1:15-17).

H. Make the most of your time by focusing on your God-given roles and responsibilities within your condition and circumstances (Rom. 12:3-8, 1 Peter 4:10).

I. Give thanks for your condition and circumstances, knowing God will use them to bring about His glory and our good through our condition and circumstances (Rom. 8:28, 1 Thess. 5:18).

J. You must accept God's redemptive agenda in the matter and embrace it, knowing that whatever happens will work out to your progressive sanctification (Rom. 8:28-29).

The Fear of Man

Proverbs 29:25

I. What is the Fear of Man?

A. To fear and revere other people above God.

B. To respect humans as God.

C. To depend on other people as the source of life.

II. What Do We Fear from Other People?

A. We fear being exposed (John 3:19-21).

B. We fear being rejected (John 12:42-43).

C. We fear being physically hurt or oppressed (Gen. 12:11-13).

D. We fear being denied what we desire (John 12:42-43).

III. Why Do We Fear Man?

A. We lack genuine love for God and others (John 14:21, 1 John 4:18-21).

B. We believe humans are the means to satisfy our needs and desires (Jer. 17:5-6, Jas. 4:1-3).

C. We believe other people are the source for solving or creating our problems (Prov. 29:26).

D. We are preoccupied with what people can do to us above what God can do to us (Matt.10:28-31).

IV. Implications of the Fear of Man

A. To the extent people believe that humans' thoughts, behaviors, and actions are the source or solution to their needs, desires, and problems is the degree to which they may seek favor or approval or bow down to others to obtain their desire or to keep from losing what they currently have (John 12:42-43, Prov. 29:25-26, Rom. 1:18-25).

B. To the extent people believe that humans' thoughts, behaviors, and actions are the source or solution to their needs, desires, and problems is the degree to which they may try to deceive or lie to others to obtain their desire or to keep from losing what they have (1 Sam. 15:1-35).

C. To the extent people believe that humans' thoughts, behaviors, and actions are the source or solution to their needs, desires, and problems is the degree to which they may try to control or manipulate others to obtain what they desire or to keep from losing what they have (Esther 3:1-7:10).

V. Questions We Must Consider

A. What is it that you need?

B. Who do you believe is responsible for supplying that need?

C. Who are you depending on to meet that need?

D. What actions do you take to meet that need?

E. How do you respond when your need goes unmet?

F. Is what you call a need truly a need, or is it a desire you have elevated to a demand?

G. Can you love God and love your neighbor without it?

H. Is it something that the Bible would validate as a need?

I. Is it something that keeps you bound to the thoughts, behaviors, and actions of other people in order to have it?

J. Is it possible that you have elevated a desire to a demand, which has turned into a lust that now feels like a need?

VI. Desires We Elevate to Demands, which Turn into Lusts that Feel like Needs, Lead Us into the Fear of Man.

A. To be in control

B. To be loved

C. To be accepted

D. To be understood

E. Never to be hurt or disappointed

F. To be respected

G. To be served

H. To have personal preferences accommodated at all times

I. To be viewed as competent

J. To be approved of

K. To belong to someone

L. To be held in high regard

M. To be significant

N. To be fulfilled

O. To be satisfied

P. To be valuable to others

Q. To maintain a favorable position with others

R. To be secure and safe

S. Never to be alone

VII. How Do We Overcome the Fear of Man?

A. Identify the fears that have consumed your time.

B. Identify the desires that always lurk behind the fears (e.g., Fear of rejection = Desire for approval).

C. Identify the people, places, things, and situations you believe are the source and the solution to your needs, desires, and problems.

D. Examine the Scripture to see if your belief in the items listed in C lines up with how the Scripture says you need to love God and love others (Luke 10:38-42, 1 Tim. 6:6-8, Matt. 4:1-11).

E. Confess and repent of trying to control the uncontrollable (Job 38-42, Prov. 28:13-14).

F. Confess and repent of making people, places, and outcome of events the idols of your heart (Ezek. 14:1-11).

G. Minimize your focus on what people think of you (1 Cor. 4:3).

H. Maximize your focus on what God thinks of you (1 Cor. 4:4).

I. Study, learn, and accept the sovereignty of God in all things (Eccles. 3:1-11, 7:13-14, 9:1, 11:5; Col. 1:15-17).

J. Accept the fact that you will have to give an account of your life to God and not to people (1 Cor. 4:5, Rom. 14:10-12, 2 Cor. 5:10, Eccles. 12:13-14).

K. Accept the fact that every good and perfect gift is from God and not people (Jas. 1:16-17).

L. Accept the fact that all that you need comes from God and not people (2 Peter 1:1-3, Phil. 4:19, Rom. 8:31-32, Ps. 145:8-16, Heb. 4:16).

M. Look to God for justice and not to people (Prov. 29:26, Rom. 12:19).

N. Don't insist that people live a life to please you; insist they live a life to please God (Gal. 1:10, 1 Cor 10:31).

O. Humble yourself and submit to the doctrines/disciplines/duties of the Christian faith (2 Peter 1:1-10, 1 Peter 4:10, Rom. 12:1-21, 2 John).

P. Practice serving people according to God's will and not according to how you feel or what you want from them in return (1 Cor. 13:1-8, Rom. 12:9-21, John 13:34-35, Luke 6:31-38).

Q. Practice setting your mind on God's agenda in every aspect of your life and seek to live according to that agenda (Matt. 6:33, Col. 3:1-25, Eph. 5:1-18).

The Fear of Man Checklist

Place a check by the things you see yourself doing.

_____ Giving in to peer pressure

_____ Having difficulty saying no to others

_____ Being consumed with what you perceive you need from others.

_____ Being consumed with what you don't want from others

_____ Justifying your mistakes to others

_____ Second-guessing decisions because of what others may think

_____ Getting embarrassed

_____ Telling lies to cover up

_____ Anger (due to not getting what you want or getting what you don't want)

_____ Preoccupation with how you look

_____ Avoiding others or isolating self from others

_____ Feeling good or bad about yourself according to the standards of people around you

_____ Constantly comparing yourself to others

_____ Avoiding sharing your faith

_____ Compromising your beliefs because of the setting you are in

_____ Feeling controlled by the thoughts, behaviors, and actions of others

_____ Spending a lot of time focusing on what others can or will do to you

_____ Spending a lot of time focusing on what others will not do for you

_____ Constantly trying to measure up to standards set by people

_____ Talking in terms of what you need from others instead of what you desire

_____ Inability to be happy or content unless certain people in your life are "meeting your needs" or satisfying personal preferences

_____ Constantly trying to protect yourself from what people can say or do to you

_____ Remembering more about your embarrassments than your sin

_____ Remembering more about being offended, rejected, or denied than you can about offending, rejecting, and denying Jesus Christ

_____ Trying to say what you think will please or provoke others to get what you want

_____ Worrying about whether people like you or not

_____ Wanting to do things for yourself and by yourself so that people will not bother you

———————

I appreciate help in developing this checklist from insights in Ed T. Welch's book *When People Are Big and God Is Small.*

Anger / Contentment

Understanding Anger

I. The *Definition* of Anger (Eph. 4:26-32)

A. Disposition of the mind that entertains antagonism toward another individual, manifesting itself in various emotions and actions (Gen. 4:1-8, Mark 3:1-6).

B. Anger is an attitude that results in emotions that move into action (Prov. 14:17, 29; 15:18; 16:32; 19:19; 22:24-25).

C. Anger can be godly/righteous indignation—To be troubled or disgusted in attitude or action as a result of someone disgracing God or disregarding His holy laws (Ex. 32:1-30, Eph. 4:26-27, John 2:12-17, Neh. 5:1-13).

D. Anger can be worldly/sinful—To have ungodly attitudes and actions as a result of some perceived need, desire, personal preference/standard not being met by someone or being offended by someone (Num. 20:1-13; Eph. 4:31-32; 1 Sam. 18:6-8, 20:24-34; Jas. 1:19-20; Matt. 5:21-22).

II. The *Deliberation* on Righteous Indignation vs. Worldly/Sinful Anger (Eph. 4:26-32)

A. Godly anger or righteous indignation is the exception. Very seldom are people angry about the things that disgrace God or disregard His holy laws. When people are motivated by righteous indignation, they are filled with desire to see justice done for the glory of God (not self) as they walk by the Spirit of

God. When people do act in godly anger or righteous indignation, they are commanded to deal with it before the day is over so that the devil does not use it against them to lead them into sin.

B. Generally, when people are angry it has nothing to do with someone disgracing God or disregarding His holy laws. They are not thinking about God, His holy laws, His righteousness, His will, or His ways. They are thinking about themselves, their feelings, their wants, or their needs. They are self-centered, not God-centered. They are preoccupied with what they crave, the means to the end that is not providing that object of desire, or something that hinders that craving from being realized.

C. Therefore, most of the time when people are angry, it is a worldly/sinful anger of man. What they want within the situation is not granted, they are receiving something they do not want, or they are not receiving what they want from a person.

D. As a result of not receiving what they want or getting what they don't want, ungodly attitudes and actions begin to manifest. Instead of being thankful to God for how He will use the situation or accepting what God has allowed in the situation, they become negative and ungodly in thoughts, words, actions, and relational patterns.

III. The *Details* of Life That Can lead to Worldly/Sinful Anger

A. Misplaced dependence—depending on people, places, things, or events to provide what only God provides

B. Unrealistic expectations—expecting things that are beyond the scope of possibility

C. Lack of training in handling disappointments—not accepting the fallibility of people, places, things, and events

D. Not accepting powerlessness over people, places, outcomes of events—resisting the fact that we were not designed to control people and the outcome of events

IV. The *Desires* That Become *Demands* of the Heart as the Source of Worldly/ Sinful Anger (Jas.4:1-2)

A. When your desire to be affirmed becomes a demand to be affirmed, worldly/ sinful anger of man results.

B. When the desire not to be put down by others becomes a demand not to be put down by others, worldly/sinful anger of man results.

C. You walk in worldly/sinful anger when you demand _____ and do not get it:

1. To have control, To be loved, To be accepted, To be understood

2. Never to be hurt again, To be respected, To be served, To have your way

3. To be viewed as competent, To be approved of, To belong to someone

4. To be held in high regard, To maintain a favorable position with people

D. When the desire for people to do or handle things your way or for life to go your way becomes a demand, worldly/sinful anger results when your demands are not met.

V. The *Different* Expressions of Worldly/Sinful Anger (Eph. 4:31)

A. Bitterness—resentment

B. Wrath—intense fury or rage

C. Anger—deep-seated hostility within the heart toward another

D. Clamor—verbal fighting with people

E. Slander—ugly words, mean words in reference to someone's reputation, verbal abuse in reference to someone's character

VI. The *Dangerous* Ways People Deal with Anger (Jas. 1:19-20, Eph. 4:26-27)

A. Suppress—acting like it does not exist

B. Aggression—openly expressing anger at someone else's expense

C. Passive-aggressive—indirectly expressing anger at someone else's expense

D. Not dealing with it before the day is done

VII. The *Direction* to Deal with Anger (Jas. 1:19, Eph. 4:31, Col. 3:1-8)

A. Acknowledge your anger.

B. Confess the sin of your anger.

C. Identify the details of life whereby you have chosen to be angry.

D. Identify the specific desires you have been demanding to be fulfilled by God, people, places, and events that resulted in your responding in anger due to not getting your way.

E. Accept your inability to control God, people, and the outcome of circumstances.

F. Accept these conditions:

    1. The other person may be willing and able.

    2. The other person may be willing and unable.

    3. The other person may be unwilling and able.

    4. The other person may be unwilling and unable.

    5. It may be a desire that was not meant to be satisfied.

G. Accept responsibility for your unloving thoughts, words, and deeds in the situation.

H. Repent of unloving thoughts, words, and deeds in the situation.

I. Choose to serve and love others unconditionally.

J. Follow the biblical mandate according to the relationship (1 Cor.13:4-7).

1. Husband/Wife (Eph. 5:18-33, Col. 3:18-19, 1 Peter 3:1-12)

2. Children (Eph. 6:1-2, Col. 3:20)

3. Parent (Eph. 6:4, Col. 3:21, Deut. 6:6-9, Prov. 22:6)

4. Friends (Prov. 27:5-6, Prov. 17:17, Prov. 27:9, Prov. 18:24)

5. Others (1 Peter 3:8-12, Rom. 12:9-21, Gal. 6:1-10)

6. Leaders (1 Tim. 4:16, Heb. 13:7, 17, 1 Peter 5:5, 1 Tim. 5:17-22, Luke 6:40)

7. Employer/Employee (Eph. 6:5-9, 1 Peter 2:18-29)

8. Government (Rom.13:1-2, 1 Peter 2:13-17)

9. Enemies (Luke 6:27-36)

K. Don't allow anger to go beyond that day (Eph. 4:26-27).

Learning to Be Content

Philippians 4:10-14

The Definition of *Contentment*: Sufficient satisfaction within the heart through the fellowship with and power of Jesus Christ, apart from external circumstances and other people

I. The *Picture* of Contentment Painted by the Apostle Paul (Phil. 4:10-14)

A. Paul rejoiced in the Lord when others came through for him, yet his state of mind was not conditioned upon their gift (v10-v11).

B. Paul learned to live with what he had and let it be enough for him (v12).

C. Paul learned to live without anticipating the provision of God (v12).

D. Paul adjusted his desires to match his condition and circumstances (v12).

E. Paul depended on God's power from within to cultivate contentment in his condition and circumstances (v13).

F. Paul had fellowship with God in his condition and circumstances (v13).

G. Paul showed appreciation when others came through for him, yet he did not live for or by what others may or may not do for him (v14).

II. The *Perspective* of Contentment Promoted in the Scriptures

A. Content people are able to accept their condition (Phil. 4:11-13).

B. Content people are able to accept their contents/finances (Heb. 13:5).

C. Content people are able to endure their circumstances (2 Cor. 12:10).

D. Content people depend on Christ (Heb. 13:5).

E. Content people are pursuing Christ-likeness (1 Tim. 6:6-8).

F. Content people are not complainers (Phil. 4:11-13).

G. Content people have an attitude of consideration (Phil. 4:11-13).

III. The *Process* to Contentment Presented in Seven Key Steps

A. We must accept what God allows in our condition and circumstances and make the most of it with no complaints (1 Peter 5:6-11, Phil. 2:14-16).

B. We must purge ourselves of the lust that drives the discontentment (2 Tim. 2:22, Rom. 13:14).

C. We must accept the fact that we are passing through this world, not settling down in this world (Phil. 3:20-21, 1 Peter 2:11).

D. We must learn to function in our God-given roles and responsibilities within our condition and circumstances (Rom. 12:3-8, 1 Peter 4:10).

E. We must no longer demand that people satisfy us but seek to help people glorify God (Matt. 5:16, Rom. 15:2-3).

F. We must give thanks for our condition and circumstances, knowing God will use them to bring about His glory and our good through our condition and circumstances (Rom. 8:28, 1 Thess. 5:18).

G. We must enjoy every pleasure that God allows, endure every pain that God allows, while living from Him, through Him, and to Him in our condition and circumstances and focusing on His covenant with us (Eccles. 5:18-20, 12:13-14; 1 Cor. 13:7; Heb. 13:5-6).

Questions to Consider this Week

1. What do I want that I cannot control getting?

_____

_____

2. What am I getting that I don't want and can't control?

_____

_____

3. How am I responding in attitude to this?

_____

_____

4. How am I responding in conversation to this?

_____

_____

5. How am I responding in actions to this?

_____

_____

6. How am I treating others as a result of this?

_____

_____

7. According to Scripture how would God view my attitude, conversation, actions, and relational patterns in relation to this?

_____

_____

8. What do I need to accept that God has allowed?

_____

_____

9. How do I need to obey God in this situation?

_____

_____

10. What has God promised in His Word that I can rest on in this situation?

_____

_____

11. How can I adjust my desires to match my situation?

_____

_____

Self-Esteem / Self-Image / Self-Love

A Biblical Perspective on Self-Esteem

I. The Definition and Understanding of Self-Esteem

A. The word *self-esteem* is not found anywhere in the Bible and therefore should be used with caution when discussed in Christian circles.

B. One dictionary describes self-esteem as a confidence and satisfaction in oneself, or self-respect.

C. The Bible does not promote the idea that we should pursue building confidence in self, being satisfied with ourselves, or having self-respect.

D. However, the Bible does present the idea that a person will feel good about himself or feel down on himself, as a result of moral choices.

E. The Bible even demonstrates that there is a confidence or fear we experience as a result of moral choices. To understand this we must discuss the conscience.

II. Understanding the Conscience

A. The conscience can be defined as the faculty of the immaterial (nonphysical) heart that judges the thoughts, intentions, words, and deeds of an individual according to the standards given it by God, governing authorities, and personally acquired standards (Rom. 1:18-20,32, 2:14-15, 13:1-5, 14: 22-23).

B. Man's conscience is an instinctual judge of his thoughts, words, and actions, accusing him when he does something that is morally wrong and excusing him when he does something that is morally right (Rom. 2:14-15).

C. The conscience is a universal entity in that all have it, whether believer or unbeliever (Rom. 1:18-20, 2:14-15; 1 Tim. 3:8-9).

III. Understanding Conscience Joy and Conscience Sorrow (Gen. 4:1-7, 2 Sam. 24:10, Rom. 2:14-15)

A. When a person makes a choice that is morally right, he can expect to experience pleasantness in the soul that comes from the conscience. This is called conscience joy and results in his feeling good about himself.

B. When a person makes a choice that is morally wrong, she can expect to experience unpleasantness in the soul that comes from the conscience. This is called conscience sorrow and results in her feeling bad about herself.

C. This state of unpleasantness and pleasantness in one's soul is not tied to a person's feeling worthy or unworthy. It is tied to being guilty of sin or clear of sin before the presence of God (Gen. 4:1-7, Rom. 2:14-15, 1 John 3:21).

IV. Understanding Confidence before God and Confidence in Self

A. When a believer walks rightly, she will have confidence before God: a sense of assurance that she is right before God and certainty that she is doing what pleases God. She will feel good about herself, and her confidence is not in herself but in the fact that she is doing what God wants (1 John 3:21, 2 Cor. 1:12).

B. When an unbeliever instinctively does what is right according to the work of the law written on his heart, he will experience conscience joy and confidence accordingly. He will feel good about himself and have a confidence in himself (what the world would call self-respect), rather than a confidence before God (Rom. 2:14-15, Phil. 3:1-6).

C. Therefore, the confidence the unbeliever has is based on lining up with the work of the law written on his heart. His confidence is not based on God's righteousness produced by faith in Jesus Christ. Unbelievers can find themselves doing right and feeling good about themselves as a result, leading to a confidence in themselves and not a confidence before God. They are living for themselves and not for God, but they feel good about themselves because at some point in their decisions in that day or time, they did something right that resulted in the affirmation of their conscience (Rom. 2:14-15, Phil. 3:1-6).

D. On the contrary, the believer will do right according to the work of the law written on his heart and the Word of God as guided by the Holy Spirit. As a result, he will experience conscience joy, as well as joy that comes from the Holy Spirit. The believer will feel good about himself, have confidence before God, and move toward God because he is driven by the Spirit of God. He is living for God and not himself, experiencing a joy that comes from doing what is right and from walking by the Holy Spirit (1 John 3:21-24, Gal. 5:16-22, Heb. 10:19-22).

E. As the believer does what is right, he will experience conscience joy, leading to feeling good about himself and a confidence before God. As an unbeliever does what is right, he will experience conscience joy, leading to feeling good about himself and a confidence in himself. Both experience the same conscience joy but go in different directions.

V. Understanding Fearfulness of the Heart (Prov. 28:1, Gen. 3:1-10)

A. When a believer does something that is wrong, he will experience conscience sorrow, resulting in experiencing fearfulness in the heart.

B. When an unbeliever does something that is wrong, she experiences conscience sorrow, which will also result in fearfulness in the heart.

C. This fearfulness is a fear of God's judgment that both believer and unbeliever experience.

VI. Bringing It All Together

A. People or circumstances cannot produce conscience sorrow or conscience joy within us. We cannot produce conscience joy or conscience sorrow within ourselves or a confidence before God or lack of confidence before God. These feelings are a by-product of our morally right or wrong thoughts, desires, words, and actions.

B. If we are thinking, desiring, speaking, acting, or reacting in sinful ways toward God, people, or circumstances, we can expect conscience sorrow that results in feeling bad about ourselves and a lack of confidence before God. If we are thinking, desiring, speaking, acting, or reacting in godly ways toward God, people, and circumstances, we can expect conscience joy that results in feeling good about ourselves and confidence before God.

C. Unbelievers do not have the Holy Spirit. They may from time to time adhere to and follow the work of the law written on their hearts or some standard in line with that work of the law. As a result, they can expect conscience joy, resulting in feeling good about themselves, and have a confidence in themselves, resulting in drawing near to a false god and believing it's the true God. However, when unbelievers do what is wrong, they can expect conscience sorrow, resulting in feeling bad about themselves, lacking confidence before God, and lacking confidence within themselves.

D. Believers have the Holy Spirit. When believers walk by the Holy Spirit, they will experience conscience joy and the joy of the Holy Spirit, resulting in feeling good about themselves, having confidence before God, and drawing near to Him. Believers and unbelievers both experience conscience joy and conscience sorrow, but each group follows a different path. Unbelievers do not experience the joy of the Holy Spirit; they are not Christians and cannot walk by the Holy Spirit or experience the benefits thereof.

E. The dictionary defines *self-esteem* as a confidence and satisfaction in oneself, or self-respect, without describing how one comes to this self-satisfaction or self-respect.

F. We present a biblical counterpoint, which demonstrates that making morally right or wrong choices results in the conscience, producing:

1. conscience joy (as a result of one's making a morally right choice)

   a. which then leads one to feeling good about oneself (as a result of making a morally right choice).

   b. which then leads to the confidence before God for believers / confidence in self for unbelievers (i.e., self-respect) when making morally right choices.

2. conscience sorrow (as a result of one's making a morally wrong choice)

   a. which then leads one to feeling bad about oneself (as a result of making a morally wrong choice).

   b. which then leads to a lack of confidence before God for believers / a lack confidence in self for unbelievers (i.e., lack of self-respect) when making morally wrong choices.

The Big Picture of Conscience Joy and Conscience Sorrow
Conscience joy and conscience sorrow are universally experienced by both believer and unbeliever.
When believers do what is right, they will experience conscience joy, resulting in feeling good about themselves.
When unbelievers do what is right, they will experience conscience joy, resulting in feeling good about themselves.
When believers do what is right, they will experience a confidence before God.
When unbelievers do what is right, they will experience a confidence in themselves.
When believers do what is wrong, they will experience conscience sorrow, resulting in feeling bad about themselves.
When unbelievers do what is wrong, they will experience conscience sorrow, resulting in feeling bad about themselves.
When believers do what is wrong, they will experience a lack of confidence before God.
When unbelievers do what is wrong, they will experience a lack of confidence in themselves and before God.
Feeling down on self or feeling good about self is a by-product of morally right or wrong choices. Therefore, we can gain a basic understanding of the moral choices that have been made by individuals through evaluating their experiences of conscience joy and conscience sorrow.
This can become a tool for evaluation, as opposed to a tool for self-worship.

VII. In the worst case, an unbeliever can have conscience joy but can sear or numb his conscience to conscience sorrow (Rom. 1:28-32, Eph. 4:17-19).

A. As a nonbeliever sears or numbs his conscience, he no longer feels the conscience sorrow (Rom. 1:32, Eph. 4:17-19, 1 Tim. 4:1-2).

B. The nonbeliever experiences conscience joy but not the conscience sorrow that comes from wrongdoing, because he has numbed or seared his conscience to the feelings of guilt that bring the conscience sorrow. He is aware of his guilt before God but is not experiencing the conscience sorrow with the awareness (Rom. 2:14-15, Eph. 4:17-19, Rom. 1:28-32, 1 Tim. 4:1-2).

C. The nonbeliever experiences the peace that the world gives but not the conscience sorrow that comes from wrongdoing, because she has numbed or seared her conscience to the feelings of guilt that bring the conscience sorrow. She is aware of her guilt before God but is not experiencing the conscience sorrow with the awareness (John 14:27, Eph. 4:17-19, 1 Tim. 4:1-2).

Key Point: Where the secular world speaks of self-esteem, we replace that concept with the biblical perspective of conscience joy and conscience sorrow. The world promotes self-esteem as something to pursue, but biblically we recognize it as a by-product of moral choices and as more appropriately described as conscience joy and conscience sorrow. The biblical counterpoint to secular self-esteem becomes a tool for evaluation, as opposed to an avenue for self-worship.

A Biblical Perspective on Self-Image

I. Worldly vs. Biblical Perspectives on Self-Image

A. A dictionary describes *self-image* as one's perception of oneself or one's role. This has to do with who we believe we are and who we believe we are not. It also reflects what we believe our roles are in life.

B. Secular humanistic understanding of self-image could lead us to believe that we have the option to define or redefine who we are according to what we believe.

C. When God created us, He had a specific design and order for us to operate in as man and woman (Gen. 1:26-30). From the very beginning, the first man and woman rejected that design and order, deciding to follow their own understanding of life and creation (Gen. 3:1-10). As a result, self-image has become an amalgamation of ideas that keep individuals focused on defining and redefining themselves as they see fit.

D. From a biblical perspective, self-image is not something defined or redefined by each person's ideas about himself. Self-image is prescribed by what God has said to be true about each person. Therefore, he must look to God to understand who he is, who he is not, and what he is to become (Rom. 12:2-3).

E. If a person does not have the view of himself that aligns with what God says is true about him, he has a false view of himself and thinks more highly of himself that he ought to think (Rom. 12:3).

F. In order to understand self-image through a biblical perspective, we must first look at the biblical concepts of pride and humility.

II. Understanding Pride (Ps. 10:3-4, Rom. 8:5-7, Acts 12:21-23, and Dan. 4:30-32)

A. Pride can be defined as a mind set on self with resistance to the will of God.

B. A prideful person raises his standard for thinking, speaking, and behaving above God's standard.

C. A prideful person has a view of himself based on his own opinions and the opinions of others, apart from the truth of God's Word.

D. Pride leads us to have an improper view of ourselves, leading to our own destruction.

III. Understanding Humility (John 3:26-30; Rom. 12:3, 8:5-7)

A. Humility is a mind set on Christ with submission to the will of God.

B. Humility is embracing a view of one's self according to the standards of God and not the opinions of other people or one's own views.

C. A humble person adjusts his standards to align with the will of God.

D. Humility leads us to have a proper view of ourselves, leading to a life of stability.

IV. A Dictionary's Description of Self-Image and a Biblical Perspective

A. The dictionary defines self-image as a person's perception of himself.

B. The dictionary also describes self-image as a person's perception of his roles in life.

C. The question is how does a person come to an understanding of who he is? Does he embrace the standards of God to define who he is and who he is not? Or does he embrace his own ideas, the culture's ideas, or others' ideas? If he embraces his own ideas, the culture's ideas, or others' ideas, he is embracing the doctrine of the secular culture and showing preoccupations with the flesh.

D. A person's self-image is not high or low but right or wrong. Self-image ultimately is an issue of pride and humility. If a person is walking in pride, he will have the wrong self-image. If he is walking in humility, he will have the right self-image.

V. 1 Corinthians 4: 1-4 and Luke 18:9-14: Examples of a Right and Wrong Self-Image

A. In 1 Cor. 4:1-4, we see that Paul understood who he was and who he was not, according to what God established as the definitive view of himself. He aligned himself to function according to what God established. The word *humility* was not stated, but the concept of humility was demonstrated in this passage.

B. In the parable in Luke 18:9-14, Jesus presents the danger of what happens when people trust in themselves that they are righteous, thereby demonstrating walking in pride and the consequences that follow. It also demonstrates what happens when people have a right view of themselves based on the truth of God (i.e., humility) and the consequences that follow.

C. If a person pridefully builds his self-image on opinions of himself, the opinions of others, or the standards of the culture, he will have a wrong self-image. This person will ultimately be trusting in other people and his own flesh to understand himself. This will lead him away from truth and from God (Jer. 17:5-6). This person will be walking in earthly, natural, demonic wisdom (Jas. 3:13-16).

D. If a person humbly builds his self-image according to what God says is true about him in Scripture, he will have a proper self-image. This person ultimately will be trusting in Jesus Christ to explain who he is and who he is not (John 8:31-32). This person will be walking in heavenly, spiritual, godly wisdom (Rom. 12:2-3).

VI. Developing a Proper Self-Image (Rom. 12:3, Luke 18:9-14, 1 Cor. 4:1-4)

A. A person must understand who she is according to God's standards.

B. A person must understand who she is not according to God's standards.

C. A person must not allow herself to be defined by her own standards.

D. A person must not allow herself to be defined by the standard of others.

Key Point: Notice that self-image comes from a different perspective than conscience joy and conscience sorrow. Where conscience joy and conscience sorrow focus on how we feel about ourselves as a result of choices we have made, the concept of self-image focuses on what we believe is true about ourselves in relation to God, people, and situations. This gets into our perspective of who we believe we are and who we believe we are not. A Christian is united with Jesus Christ (Rom. 6:1-23). That union provides a Christian with grace to overcome sin and live victoriously for Jesus. Consequently, every Christian has the ability through the power of God to put off the improper view of himself that leads to a life of sin. Moreover, every Christian has the ability through the power of God to put on a proper view of himself so that he may live a life of victory for Jesus. As a Christian develops a proper view of self, he will come to terms with the reality that in Christ he is different than he used to be. In addition, he is now what he never was. According to Scripture, this person has been justified in Christ (Rom. 5:1). He has also been made a new creature (2 Cor. 5:17). Therefore, Christians are encouraged to live according to who they are in Christ instead of what they were in Adam (Col. 3:1-17). When viewing self-image from a biblical perspective, we use self-image as a tool for evaluation, as opposed to an avenue of self-worship.

A Biblical Perspective of Self-Love

I. Evaluating the Concept of Self-Love

A. We've all heard many clichés about loving ourselves. "You can't love anyone else until you learn to love yourself" is often said with a nod of certainty, as though everyone knows it's true.

B. The concept that loving others requires me to love myself first contradicts Jesus's assertion that the two greatest commandments are to love God and love others (Matt. 22:36-39). This passage describes two great commandments, not three.

C. From Genesis in the Old Testament through Revelation in the New, God has never asked us to love ourselves. Love for self is an implied reality.

D. A dictionary definition of *self-love* is an appreciation of one's own worth, proper regard and attention to one's own happiness or well-being, and even an inflated love for or pride in oneself.

E. The Bible presents the description of self-love provided by the dictionary in three categories. We will call these three categories selfish self-love, self-preserving self-love, and soul-loving self-love.

I appreciate Rich Thomson's book *The Heart of Man and the Mental Disorders* for clarifying this information.

II. Selfish Self-Love (evil in and of itself): making self the priority for life, making self the central interest of existence (2 Tim. 3:1-4). This describes appreciation for our own worth and an inflated love for or pride in ourselves.

A. Notice that selfish self-love keeps us in a dangerous position of believing that life revolves around ourselves.

B. Where there is selfish self-love, we will find self-indulgence, a sense of entitlement, hedonism, and a preoccupation with autonomy.

C. There is no place for selfish self-love in the life of a Christian. Therefore, the idea that we must learn to love ourselves before we can love God and others is not true.

D. Selfish self-love is a contradiction to living for God (2 Cor. 5:14-15).

III. Self-Preserving Self-Love (not a sin issue / neutral in and of itself): the natural tendency to take care of ourselves and preserve our natural bodies (Eph. 5:28-29). We recognize that a regard and attention for our own well-being is appropriate.

A. The concept here is that everyone naturally takes care of him- or herself by instinct. When you are hungry you feed yourself. When you are in pain you seek relief. When you are thirsty you find something to drink. If you are sleepy you go to sleep. These are natural, normal things we do to look after ourselves without giving them a second thought.

B. Since a husband has become one flesh with his wife, he is to treat her the way he treats himself. As he has the natural instinct to look after himself, he should have that same instinct to care for his wife.

C. The text calls this natural instinct of looking after ourselves in this manner an act of self-love. Self-preserving self-love is not sinful! It is a normal part of your day-to-day activity. It is not wrong to feed yourself, take a bath, rest when you're tired, brush your teeth, or take medicine when you need relief or healing that can come from that medicine. This kind of self-love does not prohibit you from loving God and loving others. However, if all you do is feed yourself, take a bath, etc., and do not consider the needs or interests of others, then you are no longer operating in self-preserving self-love. You are now engaging in selfish self-love.

D. One can operate in self-preserving self-love and still love God and love others. When Jesus called us to deny ourselves, take up our cross, and follow Him, He did not mean we should not look after ourselves (self-preserving self-love) by no longer feeding ourselves or taking a bath or getting clothes for ourselves, etc. He meant we are not to be consumed with ourselves and consider no one but ourselves (selfish self-love), but rather we should live our lives for the glory of God.

IV. Soul-Loving Self-Love (wise in and of itself): a person's effort to get wisdom and understanding so that he may live righteously (Prov. 19:8). This shows a proper regard and attention to our own happiness.

A. Soul-loving self-love is essentially the attitudes and actions of a person who understands the importance of having the wisdom of God to live a life pleasing to God. People who attend to their souls in this manner will find that their quality of life is one of productivity and stability. This truth is described in Psalm 1:1-3.

B. Notice that soul-loving self-love leads a person to attend to himself but not to be consumed with himself. He feeds his mind with truth so that he may live a life discerning and living out the truth. Romans 12:2 explains it clearly: "And do not be conformed to this world, but be transformed by the renewing of your mind, so that you may prove what the will of God is, that which is good and acceptable and perfect." This person may pray for wisdom (Jas. 1:5), seek wise counsel from others (Prov. 19:20), or be guided into wisdom by the indwelling Holy Spirit as He makes the Word of God plain (1 Cor. 2:6-13).

C. A Christian cannot know, understand, and live out the will of God without feeding her soul on God's Word. So then developing in wisdom from that Word leads her into a life of discernment and productivity according to God's will.

D. Therefore, soul-loving self-love is not a self-centered, self-absorbed way of living. Such a Christian seeks to know and live within the guardrails and guidelines of God's will and ways. As 2 Timothy 2:15 says, "Be diligent to present yourself approved to God as a workman who does not need to be ashamed, accurately handling the word of truth." In order to present the Word for the sake of leading others to have lives pleasing to God, we need to feed on the Word of God to understand and live accurately and winsomely.

Key Concept: Love for self is in an implied reality. The Bible affirms that we already love ourselves. We must learn to humble ourselves and start loving God and loving others more. The problems in our relationships are not caused by a lack of love for ourselves. The problems we face in our relationships are based on a lack of love for God and others. This is demonstrated in selfish self-love. Self-preserving self-love and soul-loving self-love do not contradict or keep us from loving God and loving others. They will help us look out for others as we look out for ourselves, as well as to get to know God better through wise counsel, praying for wisdom, and illumination of the Holy Spirit as we study His Word. Whereas the world promotes self-love as a virtue to be learned, biblically we recognize self-love as something we already live in a neutral (self-preserving self-love), wise (soul-loving self-love), or evil (selfish self-love) manner, depending on the context. Dealing with self-love from a biblical perspective can become a tool for evaluation, as opposed to an avenue for self-worship.

Summary of Self-Esteem, Self-Image, and Self-Love

I. Self-Esteem: Where the secular world speaks of self-esteem, we replace that concept with the biblical perspective of conscience joy and conscience sorrow. The world promotes self-esteem as something to pursue, but biblically we recognize it as a by-product of moral choices and more appropriately described as conscience joy and conscience sorrow.

II. Self-Image: The concept of self-image focuses on what we believe is true about ourselves in relation to God, people, and situations. This gets into our perspective of who we believe we are and who we believe we are not. Every Christian has the ability through the power of God to put on a proper view of himself so that he may live a life of victory for Jesus. As a Christian develops a proper view of self, he will come to terms with the reality that in Christ he is different than he used to be. In addition, he is now what he never was. According to Scripture, this person has been justified in Christ (Rom. 5:1). He has also been made a new creature (2 Cor. 5:17). Therefore, Christians are encouraged to live according to who they are in Christ instead of what they were in Adam (Col. 3:1-17).

III. Self-Love: Love for self is in an implied reality. The Bible affirms that we already love ourselves. We must learn to humble ourselves and start loving God and loving others more. Whereas the world promotes self-love as a virtue to be learned, biblically we recognize self-love as something we already live in a neutral (self-preserving self-love), wise (soul-loving self-love), or evil (selfish self-love) manner, depending on the context.

IV. The biblical counterpoints for secular self-esteem, self-image, and self-love are tools for evaluation, as opposed to avenues for self-worship.

Trials / Suffering / Depression

Have You Considered the Purpose of Your Trials?

James 1:1-8

I. Trials expose and develop your *faith* (Jas. 1:1-3)

    A. Expose *what* you depend on apart from God, so that you may turn from it and turn to God to build true hope in Him alone

    B. Expose *who* you depend on apart from God, so that you may turn from them and turn to God to build true hope in Him alone

    C. Expose *what* you truly believe about God in real time, so that you may make the necessary adjustments to build true hope in Him alone

II. Trials expose and develop your *endurance* (v3)

    A. Expose how you handle *delays* and teach you how to persevere and stay godly as you work through them

    B. Expose how you handle *denial* and teach you how to persevere and stay godly as you work through it

    C. Expose how you handle *disruptions* and teach you how to persevere and stay godly as you work through them

    D. Expose how you handle *devastations* and teach you how to persevere and stay godly as you work through them

III. Trials that are endured can expose and develop your *character* (v4)

A. Expose your immature and *sinful* thoughts, words, actions, and expectations toward God and lead you to replace them by developing godly thoughts, words, actions, and expectations toward God

B. Expose your immature and *sinful* thoughts, words, actions, and expectations toward others and lead you to replace them by developing godly thoughts, words, actions, and expectations toward others

C. Expose your immature and *sinful* thoughts, words, actions, and expectations toward life and lead you to replace them by developing godly thoughts, words, actions, and expectations toward life

IV. Consider these truths about your trials (v5-v8)

A. If we humble ourselves before God, acknowledge that we need Him, and do not stubbornly insist on our way, God will respond by giving us *divine* help to walk in His will through the trial. (This is a helpful concept shared by Jim Berg in his book *When Trouble Comes*.)

B. If we don't believe that God will help us, we can't *expect* Him to.

C. If we don't believe that God will help us, we will be *indecisive* about our choices, *hesitant* in our choices, and *divided* in our choices as we go back and forth between trusting God and trusting ourselves.

D. If we don't believe that God will help us, we will live a life that is *unstable*, *complicated*, and *destructive*, because we know the truth of God's Word but live by the lies of Satan's world.

V. Expectations not being realized can lead us to the end of ourselves and into building genuine *faith* in our Lord Jesus Christ, resulting in living a life prepared and prescribed by God in this life with people and circumstances.

VI. When we stop trying to fulfill our expectations through people and circumstances, we can begin to live for our *Savior* while living with others as explained in 2 Corinthians 5:14-15.

VII. When we stop trying to fulfill our expectations through people and circumstances, we can

A. Learn how to enjoy the *pleasures* God provides through people and circumstances.

B. Learn how to endure the *pain* God allows through people and circumstances.

C. Submit to the *precepts* of God in His Word according to our roles and responsibilities with people and in circumstances.

D. Focus on and hold tightly to what God has *promised* within this life and the life to come.

E. Hold loosely in our hearts and hands what we would like to see, what we want, and what we would like to have happen that is not promised by God from people and circumstances, so that we can live a life of faith as prescribed and provided by God.

VIII. Faith should be in

A. The *reality* of God

B. The *reformation* of our existence in totality to reflect the character of Jesus Christ.

C. The *responsibility* of God to provide, protect, and prepare us for the next life.

D. The *rewards* of God in this life and the life to come.

E. The *return* of Christ and His glory along with the *residence* created by our Lord and Savior Jesus Christ when He returns for us.

IX. Faith should not be in the *realization* of all of what we want through people and circumstances.

Understanding and Dealing with Suffering in Your Life

I. Definition of *Suffering*: to experience pain or distress as the result of choices within our control and choices beyond our control.

The Origin of Suffering

The Original Sin of Adam and Eve

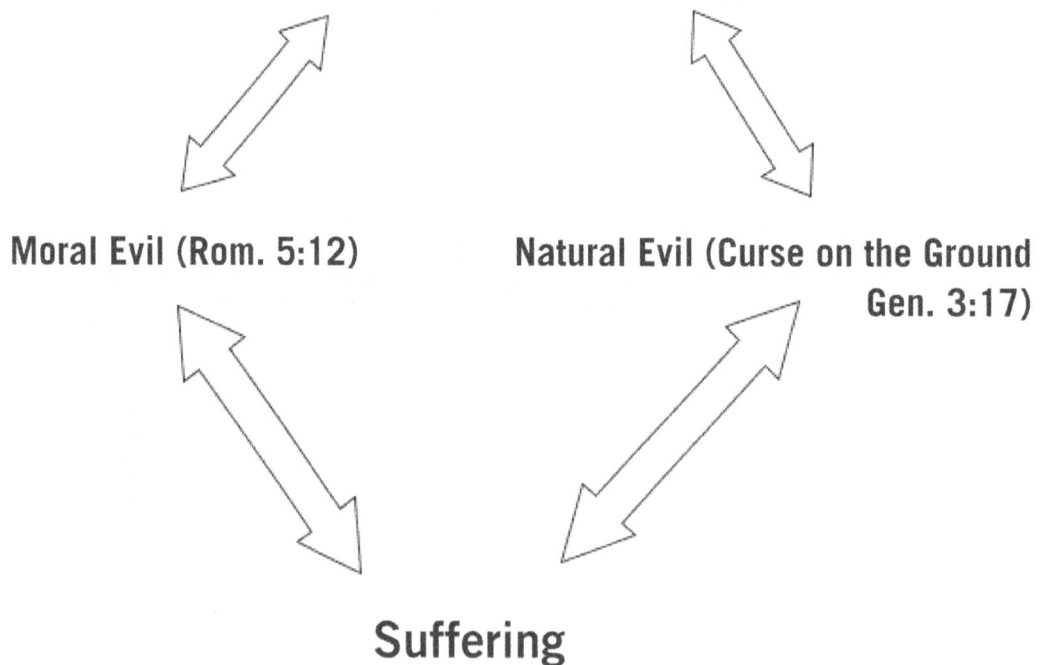

Moral Evil (Rom. 5:12)

Natural Evil (Curse on the Ground Gen. 3:17)

Suffering

II. Twelve Basic Causal Categories of Suffering

A. Sometimes we suffer because of *soil evil*: God's curse on the ground as a result of Adam and Eve's sin, resulting in all sorts of natural disasters (Gen. 3:17, Rom. 8:20-22, Job 1:19). (The creation was subjected to futility; hence great winds struck the homes of Job's children, leading to their death.)

B. Sometimes we suffer as a result of *situational evil*: malfunction of manmade items. (Luke 13:4-5). (Eighteen died from the tower in Siloam falling on them.)

C. Sometimes we suffer as a result of *sickness*: physical ailments and issues that limit or cause discomfort in the natural movement and function of the body (Matt. 9:12).

D. Sometimes we suffer as a result of the *sin of self*: disobedience to God in all aspects of life (Gal. 6:7-8, Ps. 38:1-18). (Walking in the flesh brings corruption; the unrepentance of David led to suffering in the flesh.)

E. Sometimes we suffer as a result of the *sin of others*: disobedience of others resulting in negative consequences in our lives (Ps. 119:161, 1 Sam. 26:17-25). (David was persecuted by Saul.)

F. Sometimes we suffer as a result of *Satan*: the enemy seeking to kill, steal, and destroy (Luke 22:31). (Satan sought to sift Peter, not to bless him but to hurt him.)

G. Sometimes we suffer as a result of coming to *salvation*: the flesh, the world, and the devil seeking to keep one from embracing the salvation of Jesus Christ through some sort of pain or distress (1 Thess. 1:5-7). (The Thessalonians received the word in much tribulation.)

H. Sometimes we suffer as a result of pursuing *sanctification*: pain or distress that has come to motivate biblical change or as a result of biblical change (Heb. 12:11, 1 Peter 4:1-3) (No discipline seems joyful but after one is trained from it, one develops in righteousness. As one seeks to walk in what is right, one will suffer in the flesh.)

I. Sometimes we suffer as a result of *serving*: being used by God as a vessel of honor to be productive for the advancement of His Kingdom in all aspects (2 Tim. 4:14-15, Matt. 5:11-12). (Alexander the coppersmith did much harm to Paul as Paul was serving God. You are blessed when insulted, persecuted, or someone falsely accuses you as a result of serving Jesus Christ.)

J. Sometimes we suffer to keep us from *self-importance*: to keep us from exalting ourselves, we may suffer some form of pain (2 Cor. 12:7). (Because Paul was given so much revelation, God sent a messenger of Satan to torment him, a thorn in the flesh to keep him from exalting himself.)

K. Sometimes we suffer to discover and demonstrate the *soundness of our faith*: going through various kinds of trials and tribulations so that we may see how strong or weak our faith is in Christ our King and to change or to continue in that faith, resulting in receiving the prize of our faith (1 Peter 1:5-9). (Saints were suffering through various trials, and their faith demonstrated love, belief, and rejoicing.)

L. Sometimes we suffer as result of God *snipping* us: God may prune our character to make us more productive in bearing fruit for Him (John 15:2). (God pruned the disciples that they might bear more fruit for the Kingdom of God.)

III. The Right Perspective to Consider When Suffering

A. We must embrace the fact that God is in *control* of all suffering (Eccles. 7:13-14, 9:1).

B. We must embrace the fact that we will *not escape* from the experience of suffering in this lifetime (John 16:33).

C. We must embrace the fact that God has already undergone the *worst* of all suffering on our behalf (2 Cor. 5:21, 1 Peter 2:21-25).

D. We must embrace the fact that God the Son and the God the Holy Spirit are praying on behalf of individuals who *belong* through Jesus Christ to God the Father (Rom. 8:26-27, Heb. 7:23-25).

E. We must embrace the fact that God will bring *good* (transformation of character into the image of Jesus Christ) out of suffering for the individuals who belong to Jesus Christ (Rom. 8:28-32).

F. We must embrace the fact that God will bring *comfort* to the people who are His and are suffering as a result of seeking to serve for God's will and good pleasure (2 Cor. 1:1-7).

G. We must embrace the fact that God will bring the people who are His *through* the suffering they encounter (1 Peter 5:10-11).

H. We must embrace the fact that God will inflict more *suffering* on the people who belong to Him when they refuse to turn away from practicing the sin that is currently bringing suffering to their lives (1 Cor. 11:27-32).

IV. The Right Response to Suffering

A. If we are suffering from *soil evil* and *situational evil*, we should seek to worship God as we grieve our suffering, accepting the sovereignty of God over our lives while working through the matter with endurance. We must pursue wisdom to fix, resolve, or work through the matter and seek support from fellow Christians (Job 1:19-20, Eccles. 7:13-14, 9:1; Jas. 1:1-5, Rom. 12:15).

B. If we are suffering from *sickness*, we should pray for help, repent if there is any sin tied to the sickness, trust in the Lord, and function in obedience in spite of our sickness (Jas. 5:13-15, Prov. 3:5-8). And in all feasible situations, we can seek medical support.

C. If we are suffering from the *sin of self*, we should renounce our sin, repent of our sin, renew our minds in the truth, and replace our sin with right living to restore the joy and peace to our lives (Prov. 28:13-14; Ps. 51:1-19, 32:1-11).

D. If we are suffering from the *sin of others*, we should embrace the reality that what others meant for evil, God will use to bring good to our lives while we obey God in spite of the sin of others. Where appropriate, we should confront them about the sin (Gen. 50:12, Rom. 8:28, Rom. 12:17-21, Luke 17:3, Gal. 6:1).

E. If we are suffering from *Satan's attack* to be kept from *self-importance*, we should submit to God and resist the devil with the spiritual armor given to us by God, which will cause the devil to flee from us (Jas, 4:7, Eph, 6:13-17).

F. If we are suffering from receiving *salvation* because others do not want us to change, we should become an example to others as we serve God and wait for the return of Jesus Christ (1 Thess. 1:6-10).

G. If we are suffering from *sanctification* or to demonstrate the *soundness of our faith*, we should endure and persevere, anticipating the perfect result of our sanctification and of sound faith, which is our transformation into the image of Jesus Christ and focus on the hope to be realized in Christ Jesus our Lord (Jas. 1:1-5, Rom. 8:28-29, Rom. 5:1-5).

H. If we are suffering from *serving* or from the *snipping of God*, we should embrace the fact that God will provide comfort in the midst of our affliction while we continue to serve. This will result in developing in endurance and Christ-like character (2 Cor. 1:1-7, Jas. 1:1-4).

Dealing with Depression

I. The *Characterization* of Depression: The experience of deep sorrow, hopelessness, and a sense of guilt connected to one's beliefs, way of life, expectations, and reactions toward God, self, people, life in general, and circumstances in specific.

II. The *Cause* of Depression: Depression can result from unbiblical thinking, unbiblical living and unbiblical responses (Ps. 73:1-22, Gen. 4:1-14, Ps. 38:1-18, Lam. 1:20), such as:

A. A wrong view of God, wrong view of self, wrong view of people, wrong view of life in general, and a wrong view of circumstance in specific.

B. Dealing with God, self, people, life in general, and circumstance in specific in ways that the Bible defines as sin.

III. The *Confusion* about Depression

A. Depression should not be confused with deep sorrow. Deep sorrow is the normal response to disappointment, difficulty, or even devastating life issues that is not accompanied with corresponding sin in thoughts and actions while experiencing a sense of peace (Ps. 34:8, Prov. 13:12, 2 Kings 4:8-37).

B. However, depression is a combination of deep sorrow, hopelessness, and a sense of guilt that is the result of sin in thoughts and actions (Ps. 38:1-8, 73:1-22; Gen. 4:1-14).

C. One can have deep sorrow without hopelessness and a sense of guilt while experiencing a sense of peace. However, one will not have depression without hopelessness and a sense of guilt. The experience of depression is not sin itself but the result thereof (Prov. 13:12, Ps. 73:1-22).

IV. The *Cure* for Depression

A. Identify where you may have been thinking, speaking, or acting in sin toward God in particular situations (Ezra 10:1-2).

B. Identify where you may have been thinking, speaking, or acting in sin toward others in particular situations (Gen. 50:15-21).

C. Identify where you may have been thinking, speaking, or acting in sin in response to unfavorable or difficult circumstances (Ps. 73:1-22).

D. Identify what you want or desire that you cannot control to get from God, others, or circumstances (Jas. 3:13-4:3).

E. Confess and repent of lusting after those wants or desires you cannot control getting from God, others, or circumstances (Prov. 28:13-14).

F. Confess and repent of ungodly thoughts, words, or actions toward God, others, and circumstances (Ps. 32:1-11, Jas. 5:16).

G. Identify the thoughts, words, actions, or desires God is seeking to develop through your circumstances (Jas. 1:1-8, 1 Peter 1:1-9).

H. Discipline yourself to think, behave, and relate in ways that are pleasing to God (Phil. 3:7-21, Eph. 4:17-32).

I. Identify various ways you can show thanks to God for what He is allowing in your life (1 Thess. 5:18, Prov. 17:22).

J. Lay out a daily schedule of tasks that you are responsible for doing and work on accomplishing them, apart from your feelings (Prov. 16:1,3,9; 24:27).

K. Identify some key ways you can serve others and do it apart from your feelings (Rom. 12:3-21, 1 Peter 4:10-11).

L. Focus on speaking words that are edifying (Eph. 4:29).

M. Learn to receive and cultivate hope that comes from trusting God (Rom. 5:1-5, Heb. 6:9-20, 1 Peter 1:13-16, Heb. 12:1-3, 1 John 3:1-3).

When people struggle with depression and pursue medicine for their solution or support, we encourage them to consider medicine as a temporary support but the Messiah as the ultimate solution.

Six Questions to Consider in Evaluating Our Situation

1. What is it that God wants me to come to embrace about Him in this situation?

_____

_____

_____

2. What is the biblical view of this situation?

_____

_____

_____

3. What does God want me to see about myself in this situation?

_____

_____

_____

4. What does God want me to learn about others in this situation?

_____

_____

_____

5. What does God want me to do in this situation?

_____

_____

_____

6. What will be my future service to others as a result of doing what God wants me to do in this situation?

_____

_____

_____

How to Deal with the Past

I. *Presuppositions* in Dealing with the Past

A. What has happened to you in the past is not the cause of your bondage to the past. You could not control events or other people's actions in the past (Eccles. 7:13-14; 9:1; Job 1:1-2:10).

B. Your present attitudes, words, actions, and desires regarding the past are the source of your problems with the past (Num. 11:1-6).

C. What you desire from the past situation shapes your present perspective and responses to the past (Num. 11:1-6).

D. Since memory is fallible, we tend to distort key elements of past situations (Num. 11:1-6, Ex. 5:1-23).

E. Learning your patterns of thought, words, actions, desires, and expectations before, during, and after the past experience will help you to deal with the past properly (Ps. 73).

F. God will allow or cause temporary pain in order to conform us to the image of Christ (1 Peter 1:6-9,5:10, Jas. 1:1-4, Heb. 12:5-11, Rom. 5:1-5, 2 Cor. 4:1-18).

G. An important goal of life is not to release you from the pain of your past but for you to develop spiritual maturity through the pain of your past (Gen. 50:15-20).

H. We are a product of our choices, not our past experiences. Therefore experiences are influential and not determinative. Your choices, not your past, have led you to your bondage (Gal. 6:7-8)

I. The past is from God and it exists for His glory (Is. 46:9-10).

II. The *Process* to Deal with the Past

A. We must identify what we received that we did not want in the past that we still think about with revenge, bitterness, resentment, anger, fear, or worry (Ruth 1:1-21, 2 Sam. 13:1-29). *Examples*: Naomi (which means Pleasant) wanted to change her name to Mara (Bitterness). Naomi was bitter while she was presently in the city of Bethlehem, because of her experience of losing her husband and two children in Moab. She received what she did not want from the past and held a bitter attitude in the present. Amnon raped Tamar (his half-sister); Tamar's brother Absalon held onto hatred against Amnon for two years and then killed Amnon.

1. Did we receive *rejection or rebuke* in the past that we still think about with revenge, bitterness, resentment, anger, fear, or worry in the present?

2. Did we receive *physical pain or disrespect* in the past that we still think about with revenge, bitterness, resentment, anger, fear, or worry in the present?

3. Did we receive *financial loss* in the past that we still think about with revenge, bitterness, resentment, anger, fear, or worry in the present?

4. Did we experience the *death of a loved one* in the past that we still think about with revenge, bitterness, resentment, anger, fear, or worry in the present?

5. Did we experience *abandonment from a loved one* in the past that we still think about with revenge, bitterness, resentment, anger, fear, or worry in the present?

B. We must identify what we lost or did not receive in the past that we are still treasuring in our hearts in selfish, self-centered ways in the present (Esther 3:1-11; Jas. 3:13-16, 4:1-3). *Example*: Haman's preoccupation with Mordecai's not giving him homage in the past led him to a pursuit of revenge against Mordecai from that point on.

1. Are we preoccupied with *acceptance or affirmation* we lost or did not receive in the past, to the point of trying to use God and people to gain it in the present or seeking revenge on others?

2. Are we preoccupied with *comfort* we lost or did not receive in the past, to the point of trying to use God and people to gain it in the present or seeking revenge on others?

3. Are we preoccupied with *security* we lost or did not receive in the past, to the point of trying to use God and people to gain it in the present or seeking revenge on others?

4. Are we preoccupied with *companionship* we lost or did not receive in the past, to the point of trying to use God and people to gain it in the present or seeking revenge on others?

5. Are we preoccupied with *stability* we lost or did not receive in the past, to the point of trying to use God and people to gain it in the present or seeking revenge on others?

C. We must confess and repent of the sinful choices we made in the past that have led to the sinful choices and the condition of our life in the present (2 Sam. 12:1-15, Gal. 6:7-8, Prov. 28:13). *Example*: David confessed his sins to Nathan and before God, yet though he was forgiven, he would suffer negative consequences for a long time.

1. We must confess and turn away from sinful *belief systems* about God, people, and circumstances that governed our lives in the past and now in the present.

2. We must confess and turn away from the sinful ways of *communicating* to and about God, people, and circumstances that governed our lives in the past and now in the present.

3. We must confess and turn away from the sinful ways of *living* before God and in our circumstances that governed our lives in the past and now in the present.

4. We must confess and turn away from the sinful ways of *relating* to God and to others that governed our lives in the past and now in the present.

D. We must interpret our past and live in the present according to the will of God (Gen. 50:15-20, 1 Peter 4:1-11, 1:13-16). *Example*: When Joseph had an opportunity to kill or put his brothers in jail, due to their selling him into slavery, he forgave them and told them that what they meant for evil, God had meant for good. (He interpreted his situation according to God's will instead of his past pain and lived according to God's will.)

1. We must not ask *why* God let those things happen to us, but we must ask how God is using those things that happen to us to bring about the greatest benefit to us and to others and the greatest glory to Himself.

2. We must identify those times in the past where God gave us what we did not *deserve* in blessing while choosing not to give us what we did deserve in punishment.

3. We must make present-day *choices* according to the will of God, instead of making present-day choices according to the pain of the past.

4. We must *develop* in our new life in Christ in the present, instead of pursuing the old pleasures from the past.

Dealing with the Past

In dealing with the past, we must move beyond the pain and hurt of the experience to address what we desire and who or what we worship, because this is what is shaping our response to the past. Therefore, we must take time to identify patterns of thoughts, words, actions, desires, and expectations toward God, people, and circumstances that could be hindering us from moving on from the past.

Use these questions as an avenue to examine yourself and ask God for wisdom in answering these questions. Journal your answers in a notebook or diary.

1. What has happened to you?

2. What was your reaction in thoughts, words, and deeds to God and other people in these situations?

3. What did you expect that you did not get from God, people, and circumstances?

4. What did you get that did not expect from God, people, and circumstances?

5. What was your view of God before the situation occurred?

6. What was your view of God while the situation was occurring?

7. What was your view of God after the situation occurred?

8. What do you want from God, people, and circumstances in the present so that you can get through the past situation?

9. What feelings about God, people, and circumstances arise when you think about the past situation?

10. Have you considered what God was doing when He allowed this situation to happen to you?

11. How was or is He using the situation from the past to make you more like Christ in the present?

12. What have you learned about your patterns of sin from your past situation?

13. What have you learned about the patterns of God's grace from your past situation?

14. What have you learned about God's character from your past situation?

15. What have you learned about your character from your past situation?

16. What do you need to change in thoughts, words, actions, and expectations in order to grow from the past situation?

17. What do you need to change in thoughts, words, actions, and expectations in order to draw near to God?

18. Who controls my thoughts, words, actions, and expectations?

19. Who is responsible for changing my thoughts, words, actions, and expectations?

20. Is there ever a right time to sin against God in thoughts, words, or actions?

21. Has God given me the power to obey Him in all circumstances?

22. Has God given me everything I need for life and godliness?

23. Can I truly do all things through Christ?

Decision-Making in the Will of God

I. Prerequisites to Decision-Making in the Will of God

A. *How does God speak and guide us today?* (Heb. 1:1-2; John 14:25-26, 15:26-27, 16:12-15; 1 Cor. 2:6-13; 2 Peter 1:16-21)

B. The *Sovereign Will* of God: God's comprehensive care and control of the entire world. Nothing happens unless God allows it or ordains it. This will can only be discovered in the future through looking backwards to the present. God does not give us a knowledge of this will ahead of time. The only exception to this is when God has spoken prophecy. Even then we do not get the full picture. For example, if I want to know what is going to happen within the next two minutes, or an hour, or the rest of the day, or tomorrow, I have to wait two minutes, an hour, the rest of the day, or until tomorrow to find out. God controls it, but He does not give me a moment-to-moment detail of that information. Therefore, I discover the sovereign will of God from looking backwards to the present. This will is not for me to figure out, but rather to rest in as I experience it in my life (Eccles. 3:1-11, 7:13-14, 9:1, 11:1-6; Lam. 3:37-38; Col. 1:17; Heb. 1:1-3).

C. The *Moral Will* of God: God's direction into sanctification. These are ways in which God would have us to think, desire, speak, behave, relate, serve, etc., in order to walk in a manner worthy of the Lord. We are to follow these commands in order to be holy and live a God-honoring life. God directs us in areas of life where He has determined what is right to think, desire, speak, behave, relate, serve, etc., and those areas where He has determined what is wrong to think, desire, speak, behave, relate, serve, etc. These issues are spelled out in the Bible, and the moral will of God is discovered through studying God's Word. As we study and learn what is right and wrong, we must align our lives to those standards (Rom. 12:2; 2 Tim. 2:15, 3:16-17; Ps. 1:1-3, 19:7-14; 1 Thess. 4:1-8; Titus 2:11-15; Eph. 4:17-31; Col. 3:1-25).

D. The *Non-Moral Will* of God: Areas of life where God does not give a command or prohibition. In issues that the Bible does not classify as either right or wrong, you have the freedom to decide the path you will take. However, the choice must be made in faith or the person is sinning (Rom. 14:22-23). When making decisions on non-moral issues, we must use wisdom and not allow our freedom to choose to become a license to sin (Rom. 14, Jas. 4:13-17). This will is discovered through research of the topic, wise counsel, and weighing the pros and cons of the matter, knowing that God is not going to tell us what direction to take, since He has given us the freedom to choose. However, the outcome of our decision is controlled by the sovereign hand of God. We choose but God decides (Rom. 14:22-23, 1 Cor. 6:12, Jas. 4:13-17, Eccles. 11:1-6).

II. The Big Picture of Decision-Making in the Will of God

A. We must learn to make good, godly decisions, first categorizing between moral and non-moral issues. Moral issues are spelled out in the Bible, stated as either right or wrong. With these issues we only have to decide if we will or will not obey. Non-moral issues are those the Bible does not classify as either right or wrong. We have freedom to decide the path we will take. However, the choice must be made in faith or we will be sinning (Rom. 14:22-23). When making decisions on non-moral issues, we must use wisdom and not allow our freedom to choose to become a license to sin (Rom. 14 and Jas. 4:17).

B. Some decisions are clearly stated as right and wrong in Scripture. We should decide to obey God's Word by faith (John 14:15).

C. Some decisions are made by our biblically ordained authority. The biblically ordained authorities are husbands, parents, employers, church leaders, and government. We must comply with their decisions within the parameters of their God-given authority. Therefore, God's will in those situations is that we follow the orders of the authority within the parameters given by God (Eph. 5:22-6:9, Col. 3:18-4:1, Titus 2:5-3:2, Heb. 13:17, 1 Peter 2:13-3:7, and Rom. 13:1-7).

1. We should submit even if the decisions seem unreasonable or a matter of preference (Eph. 5:24, 1 Peter 2:18-20).

2. We should submit to the decisions while communicating openly in love (Prov. 27:6a).

3. We should submit to decisions without attempting to manipulate authority. Here are some negative examples:

Open and Unloving Ways	*Closed and Unloving Ways*
Verbal anger	Physical withdrawal
Temper tantrum	Silence
Physical violence	Flattery
Making a public scene	Pouting
Nagging	Being uncooperative
Begging	Talking behind the person's back
Shaming	Sighing
Criticizing	Slowing down or stopping from giving help
Threatening	Looking sad
Bribing	Giving insincere favors or gifts
Whining	
Crying	
Refusing to do what we earlier agreed to do	

D. We should not submit to the decisions if they are in direct violation of the Word of God. Even then we should try to give a biblical alternative before respectfully declining to submit. If necessary, we accept suffering for righteousness' sake (Acts 4:19, 5:29; Dan. 1:8-13; 1 Peter 3:13-17, 4:12-19).

E. Where the Bible does not categorize an issue as right or wrong, we have the freedom to choose preferentially. These are issues that we categorize as non-moral. These issues have no moral implications; the choice is based upon your preference (Rom. 14:1-23, 1 Cor. 8:1-13).

F. Although you may have freedom to choose preferentially in issues categorized as non-moral, do not allow your freedom to become a license to sin against God by allowing that which you have chosen to lead you into sin. Let your freedom of choice be used as a license to serve God by allowing that which you have chosen to lead you into holy living, i.e., entertainment, food, job, ministry service, being a godly spouse, church worship (1 Cor. 6:12-20, 1 Peter 2:16, Rom. 14:13-21, 1 Cor. 8:4-13).

G. These decisions should be made by using biblical principles such as the following:

1. We should make sure we are controlled by the Holy Spirit (Ps. 66:18, 1 John 1:9, Prov. 28:13, Eph. 5:18, Gal. 5:16).

2. We should identify any and all biblical principles that may apply to the issue (Rom. 12:2, 2 Tim. 3:16-17, Ps. 1:1-3, Prov. 19:2-3).

3. We should seek to gather as much relevant data as possible—books, magazines, website info, etc. (Prov. 14:8,15,16).

4. We should seek wisdom and counsel from persons knowledgeable in that area in which we are making decisions. We should not try to get the person to make a decision for us (Prov. 11:14, 20:5, 19:20,15:22).

5. We should weigh the pros and cons of the available alternatives and then make a decision according to the option with more pros than cons (Prov. 14:15-16).

6. We must accept by faith that we have not sinned in our choice. We must accept the consequences that come with the choice (Prov. 16:1, 9).

7. We must accept that God will either allow it to go forward as chosen or God may re-direct as He sees fit, because we choose but God decides (Prov. 16:1, 9; Jas. 4:13-17).

I appreciate the insights on this topic from Rich Thomson, as well as from Garry Friesen in his book *Decision Making and the Will of God*.

Decision-Making Exercise

1. Identify the issue or issues whereby you have to make a decision.

_____

_____

_____

2. Determine if the issue is a moral or non-moral issue.

_____

_____

_____

3. Determine if the issue is to be addressed by those who are in authority over you.

_____

_____

_____

4. Research the Bible to see what it has to say on the issue both directly and indirectly. Write down what you find.

_____

_____

_____

5. Research any and all godly sources of information to gather relevant data on the issues. Write down what you find.

_____

_____

_____

6. Talk with people who have expertise in these issues and write down what you find.

_____

_____

_____

7. Identify the pros and cons of each alternative and write down what you find.

_____

_____

_____

8. Make a decision in faith. Write down your decision and explain why you chose that alternative instead of the other alternatives.

_____

_____

_____

Living by Purpose

Proverbs 14:8: "The wisdom of the prudent is to understand his way; but the folly of fools is deceit."

"The wisdom of the prudent shows itself in this, that he considers his conduct (וְיָבֶה as 7:7, cf. Ps. 5:2), i.e., regulates it carefully, examining and considering (Prov. 13:16) it according to right and duty; and that on the contrary the folly of fools shows itself in this, that they aim at the malevolent deception of their neighbor, and try all kinds of secret ways for the gaining of this end. The former is wisdom, because from the good only good comes; the latter is folly or madness, because deception, however long it may sneak in darkness, yet at last comes to light, and recoils in its destructive effects upon him from whom it proceeds." (Keil and Delitzsch, *Commentary on the Old Testament*)

"**Caution** is a significant element of **wisdom** (v. 8). In life, the wise person chooses the right direction because he uses **discernment** in doing so. That is, he has learned to *distinguish between* what is good and what is bad: what is true and what is false. In short, he has become adept in discerning God's will by contrasting it with all other ways. **Stubborn fools**, however, exhibit their folly not only by falling for error, but by allowing it to lead them into **deceiving** others. It is sad to note that many **foolish** persons plunge headlong into bad decisions, get involved in sinful ways and pursue empty dreams simply because they lack **caution**. Caution, or prudence, is a quality to inculcate in counseling. Most counselees need it. It causes one to stop and think before moving ahead. In doing so, he must use the Bible to help him to investigate, to contrast and to compare various options. In driving them to the Bible, caution will often bring them to Romans 14:22 and 23 in which is found the 'holding principle' (One must not move ahead until he is certain that it is right to do so). But you can't tell **stubborn fools** anything. They will persist in their ruinous ways. And, of equal import in some cases, what you say will be used to bolster their wrong views making them think that their choices are superior." (Adams, *Proverbs, The Christian Counselor's Commentary*, 105-6)

I. The Principle of Living by Purpose

A. Scripture calls for human planning while acknowledging God's sovereignty (Prov. 20:5,18, 15:22,26, 16:1,3,9, 19:21, 21:5, 24:8; Jas. 4:13-17).

B. Human decisions are to be made with the understanding of:

   1. the moral will of God—the areas of life where Scripture has stated what we are to do and not to do (2 Tim. 3:16-17; Jas. 1:19-27; John 14:21; Rom. 12:1-21, 13:1-14)

   2. the sovereign will of God—the reality that God controls all things and is working out His overall plan for the universe (Eccles. 7:13-14, Lam. 3:37-38, Col.1:15-17, Eph. 1:9-10, 2 Peter 3:1-18)

   3. the non-moral will of God—the areas of life where Scripture gives no specific instructions or commands and we are free to choose what we desire, considering our loyalty to God and love for others (1 Cor. 6:12, 8:4-13; Rom. 14:1-23)

C. Life is to be arranged according to God's priorities (Matt. 22:34-40).

D. Life is to be arranged with relationships in mind (John 13:34-35, Rom. 12:3-1).

E. Life is to be lived according to God's values (Luke 6:20-49, 12:13-34).

II. The Prerequisites of Living by Purpose

A. We must learn the character of God and His plan for humanity.

B. We must study God's agenda for every aspect of life.

C. We must become aware of our personality, spiritual gifts, natural talents, and treasures and learn how to use them to God's glory.

D. We must identify the people, places, things, and activities we are to manage.

E. We must learn where we are to lead and where we are to follow.

III. The Process of Living by Purpose

A. Identify the various roles you have in life.

B. Identify which roles you must keep and the ones you must let go.

C. Identify the biblical mandates and the responsibilities associated with each role.

D. Organize your roles according to God's priorities.

E. Identify what you are to accomplish in each particular role and the steps it will take to accomplish these things.

F. Write out the specific tasks you have to do on a daily or weekly basis to accomplish what needs to be accomplished.

G. Write out specific ways you can use your spiritual gifts and natural talents to serve your family, the Body of Christ, and other people on a daily or weekly basis.

Take some time and work through the following questions.

1. Who is God and what is His mission?

_____

_____

_____

2. What are your spiritual gifts, natural talents, and personality type?

_____

_____

_____

3. What are the various roles and responsibilities you have right now in life?

_____

_____

_____

4. Looking at your spiritual gifts, natural talents, treasures, personality, roles, and responsibilities, how do you believe God wants you to join Him in His mission?

_____

_____

_____

5. How will you prioritize and organize your roles, responsibilities, spiritual gifts, and natural talents to accomplish what God wants you to accomplish?

_____

_____

_____

6. Who has God placed in authority over you to hold you accountable?

_____

_____

_____

7. Who has God placed under your authority to hold accountable?

_____

_____

_____

8. Looking at your family's spiritual gifts, natural talents, treasures, personalities, and responsibilities, what is God's mission for this family?

_____

_____

_____

9. Looking at your family's spiritual gifts, treasures, personalities, and natural talents, what are the specific things the individuals in your family need to do to accomplish what God wants each of you to do for each other in the family and for others?

_____

_____

_____

10. How will your family do what you need to do in order to accomplish what God wants you to do for each other and for others?

_____

_____

_____

11. What will be the responsibilities of all in your family to accomplish what God wants each person to do for each other and for others?

_____

_____

_____

12. Who will hold your family accountable to do what you need to do in the family?

_____

_____

_____

13. What ministries and organizations do you need to get involved in?

_____

_____

_____

14. What ministries and organizations do you need to let go?

_____

_____

_____

After working through the information above, write a job description for each role you play and include Scripture to validate the role.

Job Description

Position Title: _____

Purpose of the Position: _____ **Scripture:**

Reports to: _____

Relates Closely to: _____

Responsible for:

_____ _Scripture:_
_____ _Scripture:_
_____ _Scripture:_
_____ _Scripture:_
_____ _Scripture:_
_____ _Scripture:_
_____ _Scripture:_

Measurable Goals for the Position

_____

_____

_____

_____

_____

_____

_____

Here are examples of job descriptions to consider:

I. Man with wife

    A. **Position title:** Husband (Head of Family)

    B. **Purpose of the position:** To lead, love, feed, watch over, protect, and serve his wife and those of the household (1 Cor. 11:3, Eph. 5:25-27, 1 Tim. 5:8, John 13:1-17, 1 John 3:16, Acts 20:28)

    C. **Reports to:** Jesus Christ, elders, accountability couple

    D. **Relates closely with:** wife, children, mother, father, mother-in-law, and father-in-law

    E. **Responsible for:**

        1. Leading the family in the direction designed by God for this family (Josh. 24:14-15)

        2. Setting an example for godly living (Matt. 5:6, 1 Tim. 4:16)

        3. Establishing a system for discipling the family to spiritual maturity (Eph. 5:25-27, 6:4; Heb. 10:24; Prov. 22:6; 1 Cor. 14:35)

        4. Providing financially to meet the basic needs of the immediate family and household (1 Tim. 5:8, 1 John 3:16-19)

5. Establishing guidelines and goals for every aspect of living in the home, according to God's standards and design for the family (1 Tim. 3:4-5)

6. Making sure each member (if Christian) of the family is connected to and serving in the local church assembly (Heb. 10:24-25)

7. Providing support and service to all members of the household in order that they may live out the purpose God designed for each individual in the household (Rom. 12:9-13, Heb. 3:12-13)

8. Protecting the family against hurt, harm, and danger (1 John 3:16, Acts 20:28)

9. Providing sexual fulfillment to wife unconditionally (1 Cor. 7:1-5)

F. **Continuing responsibilities**

1. Assisting in handling household responsibilities (Phil. 2:3-4)

2. Tracking the spiritual growth of the immediate family and household (John 21:15-17)

3. Honoring, praising, and showing appreciation to one's wife on a consistent basis (Prov. 31:28, 1 Peter 3:7)

4. Establishing and providing opportunities for family fun, fellowship, and travel (Acts 2:42, Heb. 10:25)

5. Seeking constantly to understand who one's wife is and how to serve and honor her accordingly (1 Peter 3:7)

G. **Measurable goals for the position**

1. What life skills are being developed in my life and family?

2. What needs am I meeting for my wife, children, and others right now?

3. What commitments am I keeping?

4. What household responsibilities am I maintaining?

5. What social events/hobbies have we been involved in?

6. What trips have we taken?

7. What level of spiritual maturity is found in my family?

8. Whose burdens are we bearing and needs are we meeting for one another and for those outside the family?

9. What have I protected my family from?

10. What financial provisions are being made for my family?

11. How much debt are we going into?

12. How much debt are we coming out of?

13. What goals have we set and accomplished as a family and as individuals in the family?

14. What souls have been saved as a result of our family?

15. What lives have grown spiritually as a result of our family?

II. Woman with husband

A. **Position title:** Wife (support of family)

B. **Purpose of the position:** To support and help her husband in various ways so that he may be and do all God designed for him (Gen. 2:18-22)

C. **Reports to:** Jesus Christ, husband, church leaders

D. **Relates closely with:** Husband, mother, father, mother-in-law, and father-in-law

E. **Responsible for:**

1. Submitting to husband in every aspect of life as unto the Lord (Eph. 5:23, Titus 2:3-5, 1 Peter 3:1)

2. Helping her husband in those areas of his life where he is unable to function adequately (Gen. 2:28)

3. Meeting his needs in every aspect of the marriage (Phil. 2:3-4, 1 Peter 4:10)

4. Showing respect to her husband (Eph. 5:33)

5. Keeping the home inviting and orderly (Titus 2:3-5, Ps. 128:3, Prov. 31:27)

6. Assisting her husband in the raising of children (Titus 2:3-5, Ps. 128:3)

7. Keeping herself beautiful inside and outside (1 Peter 3:3-5)

8. Providing sexual fulfillment to her husband unconditionally (1 Cor. 7:1-5)

9. Using her skills, talents, gifts, and resources to support her husband and family as first priority (Prov. 31:27, Ps. 128:3, Titus 2:3-5)

10. Being loyal, trustworthy, and dependable in attitude, action, and service to her husband in every aspect of the relationship (Prov. 31:10-12)

F. **Measurable goals**

1. In what ways am I submitting to my husband?

2. How am I using my strengths to compensate for my husband's weaknesses?

3. What needs am I meeting of my husband?

4. What ways am I showing respect to my husband?

5. Am I keeping the home inviting and orderly?

6. What ways am I helping my husband raise our children?

7. What am I doing to keep myself attractive for my husband?

8. Is my husband satisfied sexually by me?

9. What gifts, talents, skills, and resources am I using to support my husband/family?

10. In what ways have I demonstrated loyalty, trustworthiness, and dependability to my husband?

III. Child in family

A. **Position title:** Child

B. **Purpose of the position:** to obey and honor our parents according to God's standard and to glorify God by growing up into a mature follower of Christ (Eph. 6:1-13, 1 Cor. 10:31)

C. **Reports to:** Jesus Christ and parents

D. **Responsible for:**

1. Respecting them (Eph. 6:1-13, Col. 3:20, 1 Peter 1:14)

2. Maintaining responsibilities as assigned and doing what needs to be done with a right attitude (Eph. 6:1-13, Col. 3:20)

3. Supporting and encouraging them (Eph. 6:1-13, Col. 3:20)

4. Getting a clear understanding of the instructions given, which includes knowing what they expect and following those instructions

5. Maintaining household chores (knowing how to clean according to parents' standards)

E. **Measurable goals for the position:**

1. How am I showing respect to my parents?

2. How am I being supportive of my parents?

3. In what ways am I encouraging my parents on a daily basis?

4. What has been my attitude when doing what is asked of me?

5. What am I doing to develop a proper relationship with my parents?

6. What have I done recently without being asked?

7. What instructions have I been following?

8. What household responsibilities am I faithfully accomplishing?

After working through the information above, write a mission plan for your life.

Purpose of Existence (Why do I exist?)

_____

_____

_____

Objectives (What specific ways am I to join God in His mission?)

_____

_____

_____

Process (What steps do I take to accomplish what I need to accomplish?)

_____

_____

_____

Resources (Who and what do I have and need to accomplish my objectives?)

_____

_____

_____

Following is an example of my personal mission plan.

Personal Mission Plan

Purpose of Existence (_Why do I exist?_)

To lead, love, feed, watch over, protect, and serve my immediate family, those of my household, those under my care at the College of Biblical Studies, and those under my care at Jireh Bible Church.

Objectives (*What specific ways am I to join God in His mission?*)

1. Lead my family in the direction designed by God for this family (Josh. 24:14-15).

2. Set an example for godly living (Matt. 5:6, 1 Tim. 4:16).

3. Establish a system for discipling the family to spiritual maturity (Eph. 5:25-27, 6:4; Heb. 10:24; Prov. 22:6; 1 Cor. 14:35).

4. Provide financial means to meet the basic needs of the immediate family and household (1 Tim. 5:8, 1 John 3:16-19).

5. Establish guidelines and goals for every aspect of living in the home that are according to God's standards and God's design for the family (1 Tim. 3:4-5).

6. Provide support and service to all household members so they may live out the purpose God designed for each individual in the household (Rom. 12:9-13, Heb. 3:12-13).

7. Protect the family against hurt, harm, and danger (1 John 3:16, Acts 20:28).

8. Proclaim the gospel of Jesus Christ (2 Tim. 4:1-5).

9. Teach men, women, and children how to obey God (Matt. 28:18-20).

10. Equip men, women, and children to serve according to their giftedness and to relate to one another in love (Eph. 4:11-16, 1 Tim. 1:5).

11. Make sure the needs of the church and students are met (Titus 3:14).

12. Make sure the church and the classroom are pure and sin is addressed (1 Cor. 5, Gal. 6:1-2).

13. Make sure the doctrines, disciplines, and duties of the Christian faith are properly proclaimed to the church and the students (2 Tim. 4:1-5).

14. Develop and select spiritual leaders to assist in taking care of the church and the students (1 Tim. 3:1-13).

Process (*What steps do I take to accomplish what I need to accomplish?*)

1. Organize my time by my roles and responsibilities.

2. Maintain two days per week for just my wife and daughter.

3. Find faithful, available, and teachable men to groom to assist in the process of caring for the church and my students.

4. Develop a once-a-month getaway to relax and renew.

5. Find curriculum and books that I can read to help me grow in my faith.

6. Find an older man to hold me accountable and teach me according to his wisdom and knowledge.

Resources (*Who and what do I have and need to accomplish my objectives?*)

1. I have my wife to support me.

2. I have my daughter to support me.

3. I have been trained by Dallas Seminary and the Master's College and several pastors in the community.

4. I have the support of my parishioners and students.

5. I need more education in biblical counseling to enhance my ability to serve others.

6. I need an older man to tutor me in spiritual development and pastoring.

7. I need someone to teach me how to invest so that I may retire debt-free and have money to live on.

8. I need some faithful, available, teachable men that I can train to lead and take over various parts of the ministry and eventually to take my place.

After working through the information above, write a mission plan for your family.

Purpose of Existence (*Why did God allow my family to exist?*)

_____

_____

_____

Objectives (*What are specific ways our family is to join God in His mission?*)

_____

_____

_____

Responsibilities (*What is each person in the family responsible for doing to accomplish our assignment?*)

_____

_____

_____

Process (*What steps do we need to take to accomplish our assignment as a family?*)

_____

_____

_____

Accountability (*Who will hold us accountable?*)

_____

_____

_____

Measurable Goals (*How will we measure our progress?*)

_____

_____

_____

Following is an example to consider.

The Ellen Family's Mission Plan

Purpose Statement: To be a family unit that uses our God-given abilities to help each other function as God designed and to disciple other families.

Objectives of Family:

1. To bear one another's burdens.
2. To meet one another's needs.
3. To help each other grow in obedience to God.
4. To help each other grow in love for all.
5. To disciple married couples.
6. To disciple men and women according to God's leading.
7. To serve various churches and Christian organizations through our various gifts, talents, and treasures.
8. To help hurting people on a city-wide level and beyond.

Process:

1. Nicolas and Venessa will lay out monthly responsibilities according to the various roles each person in the family holds.
2. Through monthly family meetings we will discover what needs, concerns, and interests we need to address with each other and make sure that they are taken care of in a timely manner.
3. Nicolas will select the discipleship material according to individual needs of each person in the family and train each person through it.
4. Venessa will develop and maintain a family budget and manage the finances.
5. Venezia will take care of household responsibilities as assigned by Venessa.
6. Nicolas and Venessa will use their biblical counseling training to disciple men/women and married couples.
7. Nicolas and Venessa will develop a home for unwed pregnant women and a biblical counseling center to help people city-wide and beyond.

8. Nicolas and Venessa will work with local seminaries, Christian organizations, and Christian schools to teach and serve according to their resources.

9. Venezia will use her gifts, talents, and treasures to bear burdens, meet needs, and teach truth to her friends, relatives, schoolmates, and people abroad.

10. Venezia will seek to work with children via volunteering at local organizations, babysitting, and through her vocation.

11. The family will seek to have monthly times of fun and fellowship with each other and friends.

12. The family will take annual vacations for fun and fellowship.

Accountability Partners:

1. Ira and Cynthia will hold us accountable in our marriage relationship.

2. Pastor Rich will hold us accountable to living responsibly as individuals in Christ.

3. Our pastor will hold us accountable as a family to live responsibly in Christ.

Measurable Goals:

1. What life skills and spiritual truths are being developed in my family?

2. What needs and burdens of each other are we addressing?

3. What household responsibilities am I maintaining?

4. What social events/hobbies have we been involved in?

5. What trips have we taken?

6. What is our financial status?

7. What goals have we set and accomplished as a family and as individuals in the family?

8. What souls have been saved as a result of our family?

9. What lives have grown spiritually as a result of our family?

After working through the information above, develop a weekly/daily task sheet according to your roles and responsibilities.

Roles	Task for Sunday	Task for Monday	Task for Tuesday	Task For Wednesday	Task for Thursday	Task for Friday	Task for Saturday

Here is an example:

Roles	Task for Sunday	Task for Monday	Task for Tuesday	Task for Wednesday	Task for Thursday	Task for Friday	Task for Saturday
Husband	Have a talk with time to discuss some problems Go to a movie/ dinner and hang out		Make sure I take the cars to be washed			Take wife out to dinner and a movie and hang out	Help her with some of the work around the house
Father			Take my daughter to school and talk with her about her life Talk with daughter about a guy she seems to like	Take my daughter to school and talk with her about her life Discuss her progress through the book of Ephesians	Take my daughter to school and talk with her about her life Discuss the worksheet "Why Does Man Need God?"		Take daughter and friend to movie and hang out
Pastor	Finish our sermon series Try to finish Sunday school lesson	Prepare Sunday's and Wednesday's lessons Prepare for counseling sessions for today Follow up with a phone call to visitors	Prepare Sunday's and Wednesday's lessons Prepare for counseling sessions for today	Prepare Sunday's and Wednesday's lessons Prepare for counseling sessions for today	Prepare Sunday's lesson and Sunday school's lesson Prepare for counseling sessions for today		Prepare Sunday's lesson and Sunday school's lesson
Teacher		Prepare and teach Ms 4344	Prepare and teach Ms 4345		Prepare and teach Ms 405 Counseling		Prepare and teach Ms 405 Counseling
Son	Call parents and say hello						
Student		Read Ch 1 and do worksheet					

Books that helped in developing these ideas:

The Age of Opportunity—Paul David Tripp

At the Altar of Sexual Idolatry—Steve Gallagher

Changed into His Image—Jim Berg

Christian Living in the Home—Jay Adams

Created for His Glory—Jim Berg

Decision Making and the Will of God—Gary Friesen and J. Robin Maxson

Desiring God—John Piper

Discovering Your God-Given Gifts—Don and Katie Fortune

The Excellent Wife—Martha Peace

The Exemplary Husband—Stuart Scott

Experiencing Christ Within: Workbook—Dwight Edwards

How Can I Change?—C.J. Mahaney and Robin Boisvert

How Now Shall We Live? Devotions—Charles Colson

Kingdom Agenda: Living Life God's Way—Tony Evans

The Knowledge of the Holy—A.W. Tozer

Life in the Father's House—Wayne A. Mack and David Swavely

Living by Faith in Future Grace—John Piper

Lord, Change My Attitude—James MacDonald

The Mind of Christ (Work Book)—T.W. Hunt

Shepherding a Child's Heart—Tedd Tripp

The 7 Habits of Highly Effective People—Stephen R. Covey

Strengthening Your Marriage—Wayne A. Mack

War of Words—Paul David Tripp

With All Your Heart?—Nicolas Ellen

Your Family, God's Way—Wayne A. Mack

12

The Cycle of Relationships

The Cycle of Self-Centered Relationships

Pride is a mind set on self with resistance to the will and ways of God. This leads to evaluating and dealing with people according to your own estimations, leading to various relational problems (Prov. 3:5-8, 28:26, 14:12).

As you function in pride, you tend to develop a picture of people in accordance to your opinion, resulting in an inevitable cycle:

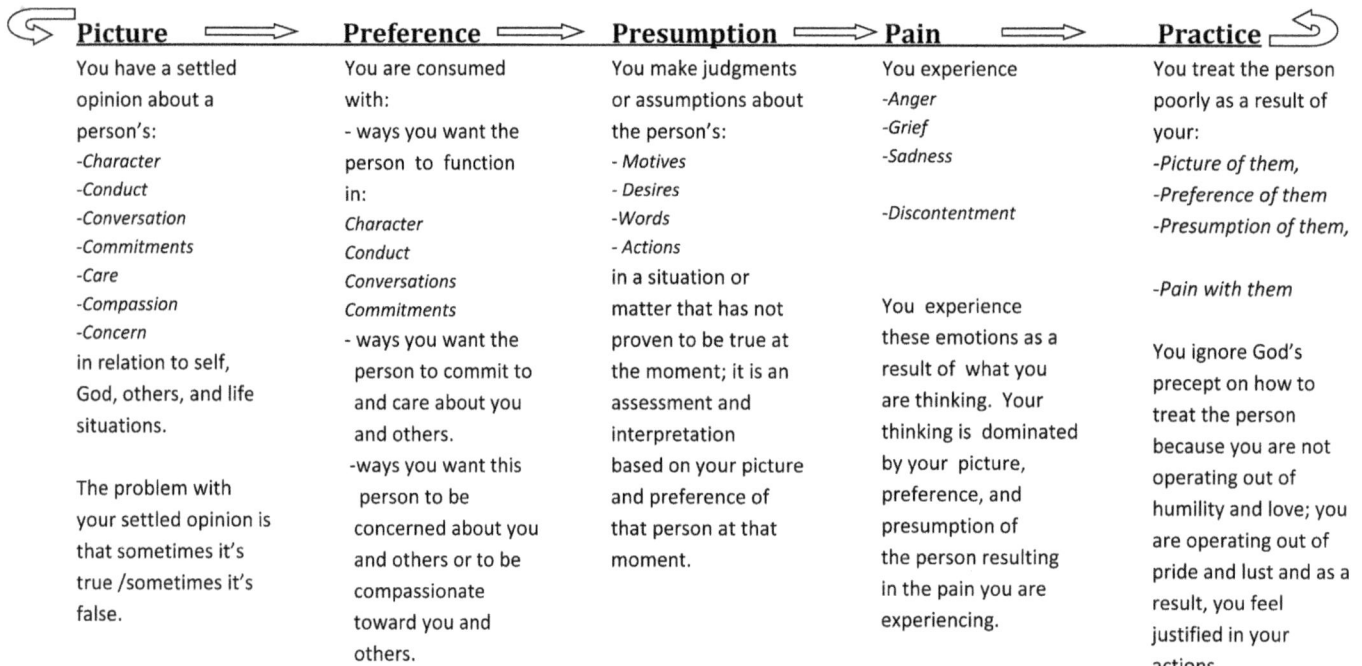

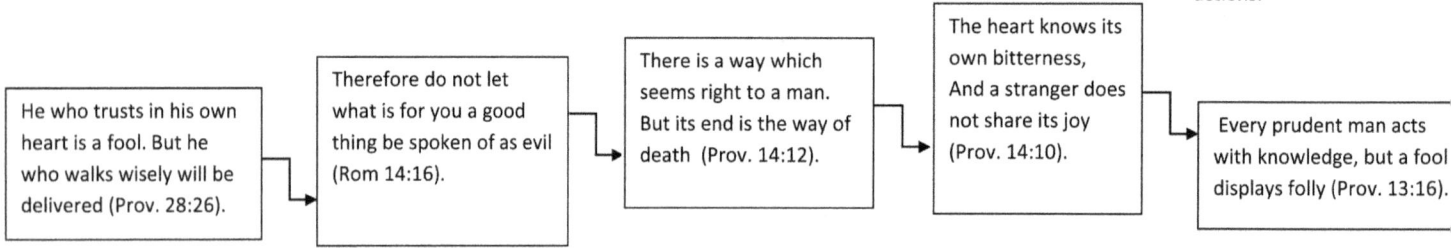

Picture ⟹	Preference ⟹	Presumption ⟹	Pain ⟹	Practice
You have a settled opinion about a person's: *-Character* *-Conduct* *-Conversation* *-Commitments* *-Care* *-Compassion* *-Concern* in relation to self, God, others, and life situations. The problem with your settled opinion is that sometimes it's true /sometimes it's false.	You are consumed with: - ways you want the person to function in: *Character* *Conduct* *Conversations* *Commitments* - ways you want the person to commit to and care about you and others. -ways you want this person to be concerned about you and others or to be compassionate toward you and others.	You make judgments or assumptions about the person's: - Motives - Desires -Words - Actions in a situation or matter that has not proven to be true at the moment; it is an assessment and interpretation based on your picture and preference of that person at that moment.	You experience *-Anger* *-Grief* *-Sadness* *-Discontentment* You experience these emotions as a result of what you are thinking. Your thinking is dominated by your picture, preference, and presumption of the person resulting in the pain you are experiencing.	You treat the person poorly as a result of your: *-Picture of them,* *-Preference of them,* *-Presumption of them,* *-Pain with them* You ignore God's precept on how to treat the person because you are not operating out of humility and love; you are operating out of pride and lust and as a result, you feel justified in your actions.

He who trusts in his own heart is a fool. But he who walks wisely will be delivered (Prov. 28:26).	Therefore do not let what is for you a good thing be spoken of as evil (Rom 14:16).	There is a way which seems right to a man. But its end is the way of death (Prov. 14:12).	The heart knows its own bitterness, And a stranger does not share its joy (Prov. 14:10).	Every prudent man acts with knowledge, but a fool displays folly (Prov. 13:16).

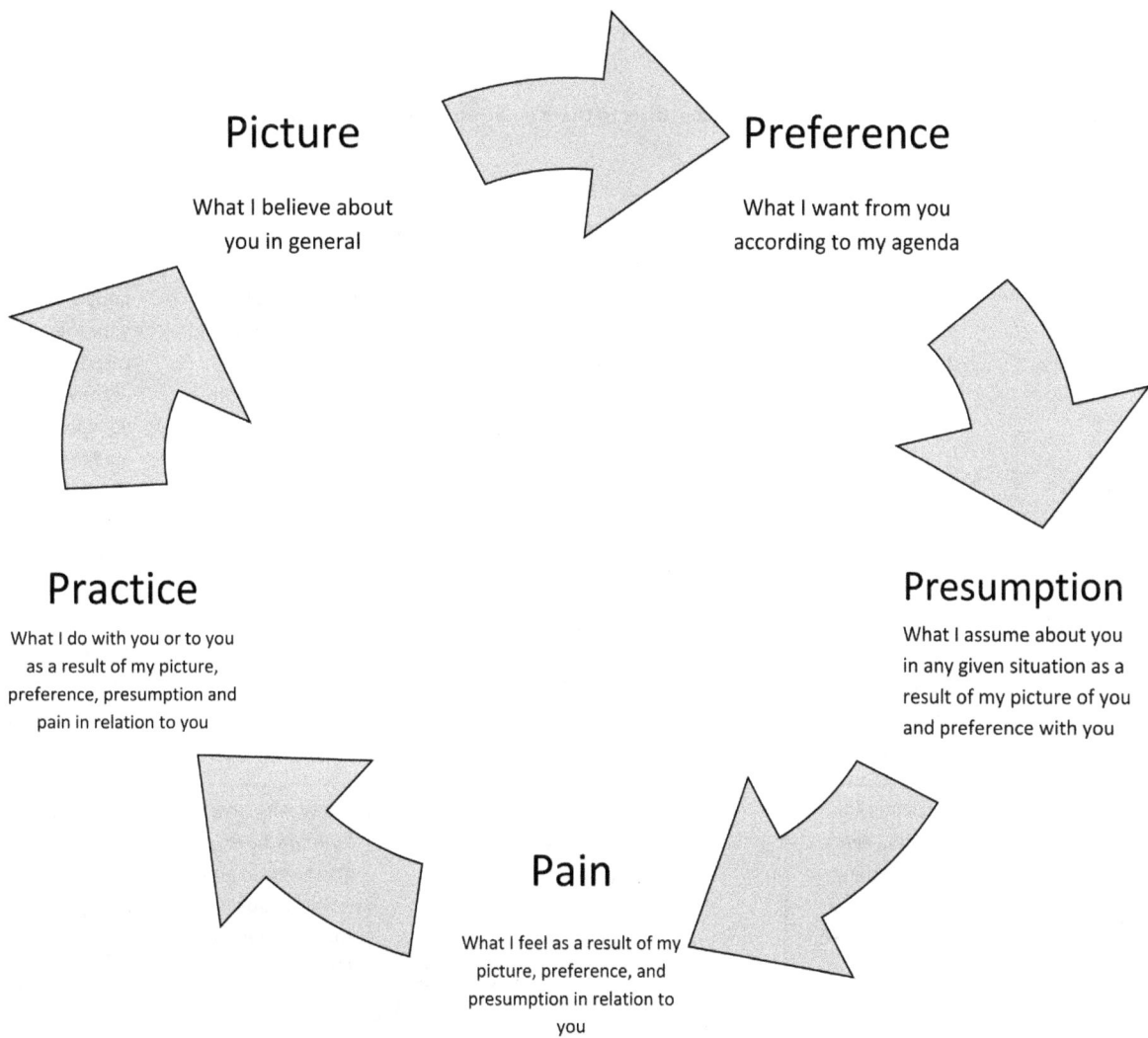

Picture

What I believe about
you in general

Preference

What I want from you
according to my agenda

Presumption

What I assume about you
in any given situation as a
result of my picture of you
and preference with you

Pain

What I feel as a result of my
picture, preference, and
presumption in relation to
you

Practice

What I do with you or to you
as a result of my picture,
preference, presumption and
pain in relation to you

The Cycle of Christ-Centered Relationships

Humility is a mind set on Christ with a submission to the will of God. This leads to evaluating life, God, and people according to the Word of God (Rom. 12:2, Phil. 2:3-5).

As you function in humility you tend to see people according to their position before God and their position before you, resulting in an inevitable cycle.

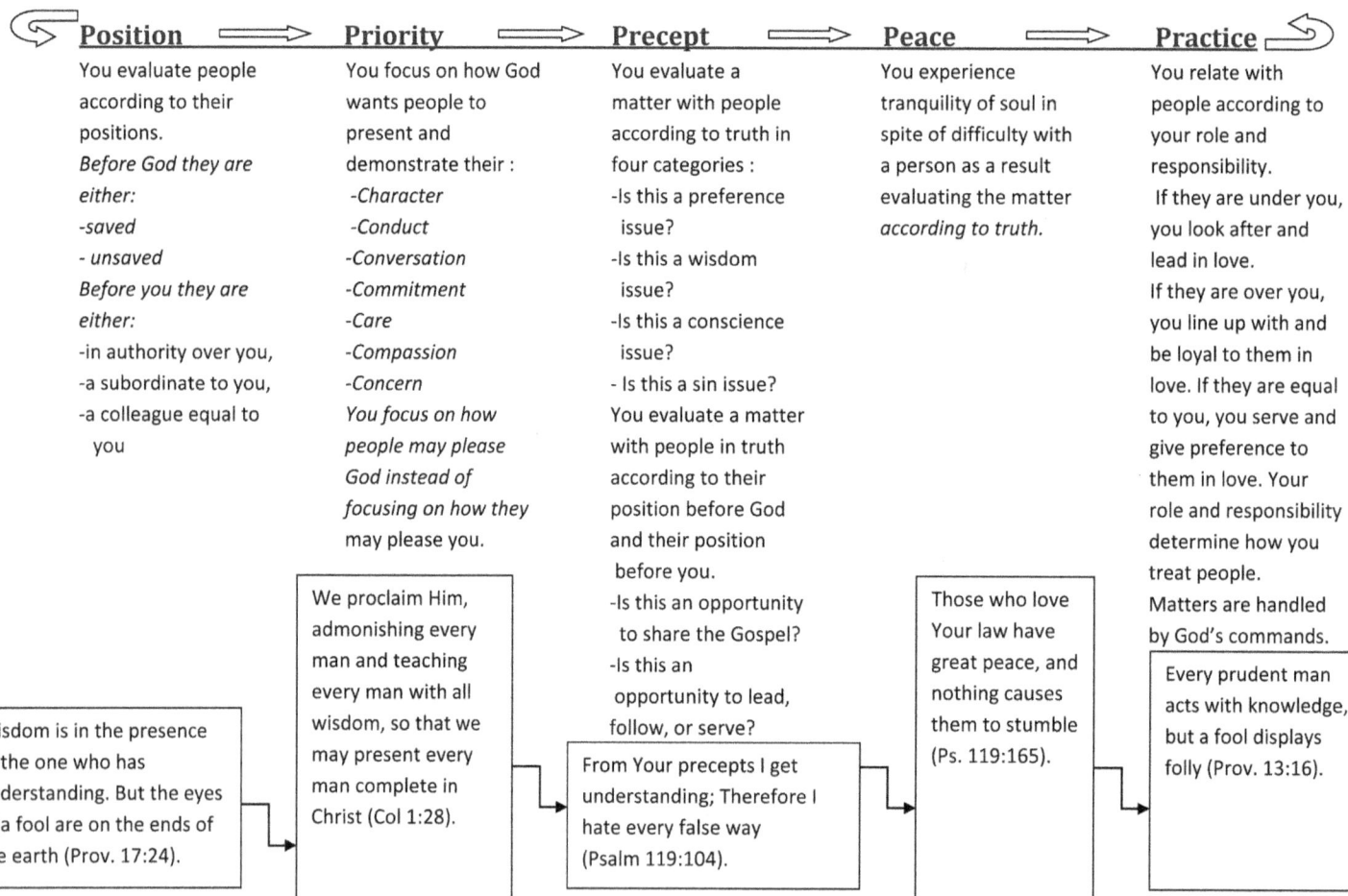

Position ⟹	Priority ⟹	Precept ⟹	Peace ⟹	Practice ↺
You evaluate people according to their positions. *Before God they are either:* *-saved* *- unsaved* *Before you they are either:* -in authority over you, -a subordinate to you, -a colleague equal to you	You focus on how God wants people to present and demonstrate their : *-Character* *-Conduct* *-Conversation* *-Commitment* *-Care* *-Compassion* *-Concern* *You focus on how people may please God instead of focusing on how they may please you.*	You evaluate a matter with people according to truth in four categories : -Is this a preference issue? -Is this a wisdom issue? -Is this a conscience issue? - Is this a sin issue? You evaluate a matter with people in truth according to their position before God and their position before you. -Is this an opportunity to share the Gospel? -Is this an opportunity to lead, follow, or serve?	You experience tranquility of soul in spite of difficulty with a person as a result evaluating the matter *according to truth.*	You relate with people according to your role and responsibility. If they are under you, you look after and lead in love. If they are over you, you line up with and be loyal to them in love. If they are equal to you, you serve and give preference to them in love. Your role and responsibility determine how you treat people. Matters are handled by God's commands.

Wisdom is in the presence of the one who has understanding. But the eyes of a fool are on the ends of the earth (Prov. 17:24).

We proclaim Him, admonishing every man and teaching every man with all wisdom, so that we may present every man complete in Christ (Col 1:28).

From Your precepts I get understanding; Therefore I hate every false way (Psalm 119:104).

Those who love Your law have great peace, and nothing causes them to stumble (Ps. 119:165).

Every prudent man acts with knowledge, but a fool displays folly (Prov. 13:16).

Position

My view of you is based on your position before God and my role in your life according to God

Priority

My agenda with you is to help you please God in all aspects of life

Precept

My evaluation of you in any given situation is based on God's perspective, not my perception

Practice

My actions with and toward you are determined by my God-given role and responsibility in relation to you

Peace

My tranquility of mind is based on my acceptance of God's agenda for me with you in the context of the matter

13

Abuse, Separation / Divorce, Remarriage

Abuse and Separation

Key Point: We cannot control what other people think, say, or do. We are responsible for how we respond to people and situations. We do not have control over a disobedient spouse. We can only control our response to a disobedient spouse. If we at any time are doing wrong to make our spouse do right, we are sinning. The end does not justify the means. Therefore, in the situation of physical abuse, the abused spouse must do what is right in the sight of God even though the abuser is not. The abused spouse is free to find safety away from the abuser without violating the marital covenant made with the abuser. Physical abuse is not biblical grounds for divorce; this is why the abused has the freedom to find safety away from the abuser without violating the marital covenant with the abuser. Separation is only permissible for a short time, to deal with safety matters for the one who is being abused and to regroup in order to face the issues within the marriage, not as a way to get out of the marriage. When people are separated they are still married. Separation is not divorce; therefore, they are still obligated to each other as a husband and wife. We cannot be separated for a long time and fulfill the commands of God in relation to the marital covenant.

I. **When people are being abused, they can work through the situation in several ways.**

A. Lovingly confront the abuser about the situation. They must make sure they have addressed their own unloving thoughts, words, or actions that may be involved in the situation before confronting the person. The abuser does not have the right to abuse another, regardless of how the one being abused may have contributed or reacted to the abuse. But people being abused still have to address their own response or contribution to the situation before confronting the abuser. If the abuser is unwilling to repent, people being abused must call in others to assist in the matter. If the abuser does not respond to this, they must call in church leaders as well (Matt. 7:1-5, 18:15-17).

B. Call the police to handle the situation (Rom. 13:1-7).

C. Find safety away from the abuser without violating the marital covenant with the abuser. Abuse is not a justification for divorce; therefore, one cannot use divorce as a way of escape from abuse (Prov. 22:3, 27:12).

D. Entrust themselves to God by doing what is right in the marriage. This means that abused persons are still responsible for doing what they are called to do within a marriage while finding safety away from the abuser (Prov. 15:1; 1 Peter 3:1, 13-17; Prov. 22:3, 27:12).

E. Married couples cannot stay away from each other for a long time and fulfill their responsibilities as a husband and wife. As long as people are married, they are called to function according to biblical mandates (see lists below). Too much time apart means that they cannot fulfill these responsibilities. This calls for repentance and return to their God-given responsibilities with each other, knowing that suffering may come in doing so. Yet people who have been abused are to do what is right while still pursuing safety. This is a difficult and delicate balance (Prov. 22:3, 27:12, 15:1; 1 Peter 2:13-25; 1 Thess. 5:18; 1 Peter 3:1-7, 13-17; Eph. 5:18-33; 1 Cor. 7:1-5; Titus 2:4-5).

II. Husbands are to love their wives (Eph. 5:25-31).

A. *Meaning*—to self sacrifice for the benefit, provision, and welfare of his wife in all aspects of her life (Eph. 5:25-31)

B. *Manner*—as Christ loved the Church (Eph. 5:25-31)

C. *Motive*—to help her to become holy and blameless; that she may function according to God's design (Eph. 5:25-31).

D. *Magnitude*—to death (1 John 3:16-18)

E. *Manifestation*—considering her interests, concerns, needs, desires, and making sure they are taken care of in the way that Christ would do for the Church; relating with her socially, spiritually, emotionally, and sexually in a manner that benefits her and reflects the character of Christ; compensating for her weaknesses in ways that Christ would do for the Church; leading and guiding her into spiritual maturity, helping her to be all of what God designed her to be in the way that Christ would do for the Church; leading her as Christ would lead the Church in all aspects of the marriage (1 Peter 3:7, 1 Cor. 7:33)

III. Wives are to submit to their husbands (Eph. 5:22-24).

A. *Meaning*—to willingly follow the leadership and instructions of her husband (Eph. 5:22-24)

B. *Manner*—as the Church submits to Christ the Lord; as if she were responding to Jesus Christ Himself (Eph. 5:22-24)

C. *Motive*—out of respect for God's design (Eph. 5:22-24)

D. *Magnitude*—in everything that is not sin, including preferences (Eph. 5:22-24)

E. *Manifestation*—following her husband's leadership and directives in all that she does in and outside the home as unto the Lord; showing respect to her husband in all aspects of the marriage as unto the Lord; managing their home in ways that are in line with her husband's leadership and directives as unto the Lord; listening to and following through on the things that concern her husband that he has requested of her as unto the Lord (Titus 2:3-5, Prov. 31:10-31, 1 Cor. 7:34, 1 Peter 3:1-6)

Considerations for Divorce and Remarriage

Key Point: As we look at divorce and remarriage, we must evaluate a few key items and evaluate what is the best course of action. Reconciliation is the optimal choice. However, people do not always do what is optimal. If a person has divorced and is looking to remarry, we must evaluate the nature of the divorce to determine if remarriage would be proper within the context of the situation.

I. **God's desire is for husband and wife to stay married.** Sexual sin was stated in the New Testament as grounds for a permissible divorce for God's people. Even then, if reconciliation is possible it should be done (Matt. 19:1-9, Luke 17:1-3).

II. **If believers refuse to stay married to another believer and get a divorce from that spouse for reasons other than adultery by their spouse, they are to stay single or be reconciled to that spouse in marriage.** If they repent and seek to return to the marriage, but that spouse has moved on, the church leaders must decide if remarriage to another Christian is possible (1 Cor. 7:10-11, Heb. 13:17).

III. **If a believer is married to an unbeliever and that unbeliever decides to leave the marriage, the believer is free to file for divorce or accept the divorce from the unbeliever.** However, if a believer has an unbelieving spouse who wants to stay in the marriage (not in the situation that he/she wishes to stay married yet live in sexual sin with other people), the believer must remain in the marriage (1 Cor. 7:12-16).

IV. **Believers are free to divorce their spouse and remarry another Christian if their spouse has committed adultery** (Matt. 19:1-9, 2 Cor. 6:14-18).

V. Believers who have been married and divorced before becoming Christians are free to remarry, since that happened before they were Christians. They are considered a new creature in Christ with new privileges to stay single or to be married to a believer. They cannot return to their formal unbelieving spouses because they are now Christians. Christians are not to marry unbelievers (2 Cor. 5:16-17, 6:14-18; 1 Cor. 7:20-40).

VI. If believers are in an unbiblical marriage, they must repent of the sin while remaining faithful to their spouses (Prov. 28:13-14, 1 Cor. 7:10-11).

I appreciate the helpful insights in Rich Thomson's book *The Heart of Man and the Mental Disorders*, as well as Bill Shannon's teaching notes in "Till Death Do Us Part."

14

Understanding Sorrow /
A Biblical View of Illness,
Psychotropic Drugs, and Biblical
Counseling

The Three Basic Responses to People and Circumstances

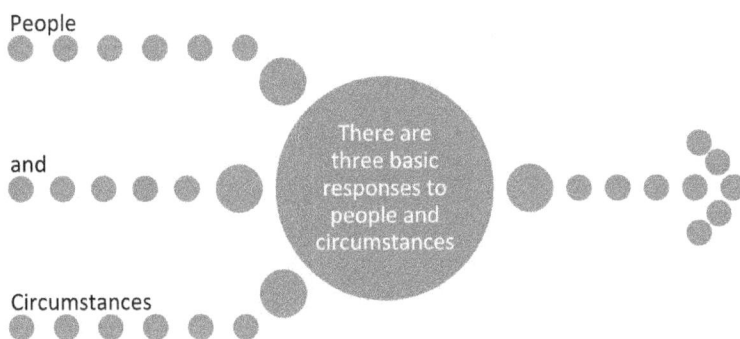

People

and

Circumstances

There are three basic responses to people and circumstances

Neutral Responses--

Demonstrating and expressing happiness, sadness, disapointment, embarrasment, or hurt that does not violate Scripture; the normal expressions in life that God does not hold against you as wrong.

Loving Responses--

to have thoughts, motives, desires, communication patterns, behavior patterns, manner of life patterns, relationship patterns, or serving patterns we are commanded and empowered by God to have that demonstrate love for God and others.

Unloving Responses--

to have unloving thoughts, motives, desires, communication patterns, behavior patterns, manner of life patterns, relationship patterns, or serving patterns that are prohibited by God and are determined by the evil in our hearts.

WHAT I CAN'T CONTROL	WHAT I CAN CONTROL
Outcome of Events Other People's Thoughts, Emotions, Desires, Words, Will	My Thoughts My Emotions, Desires, Words, Actions, Will

I AM MOTIVATED BY

Love for God ABOVE My Selfish Desires	OR	My Selfish Desires ABOVE Love for God

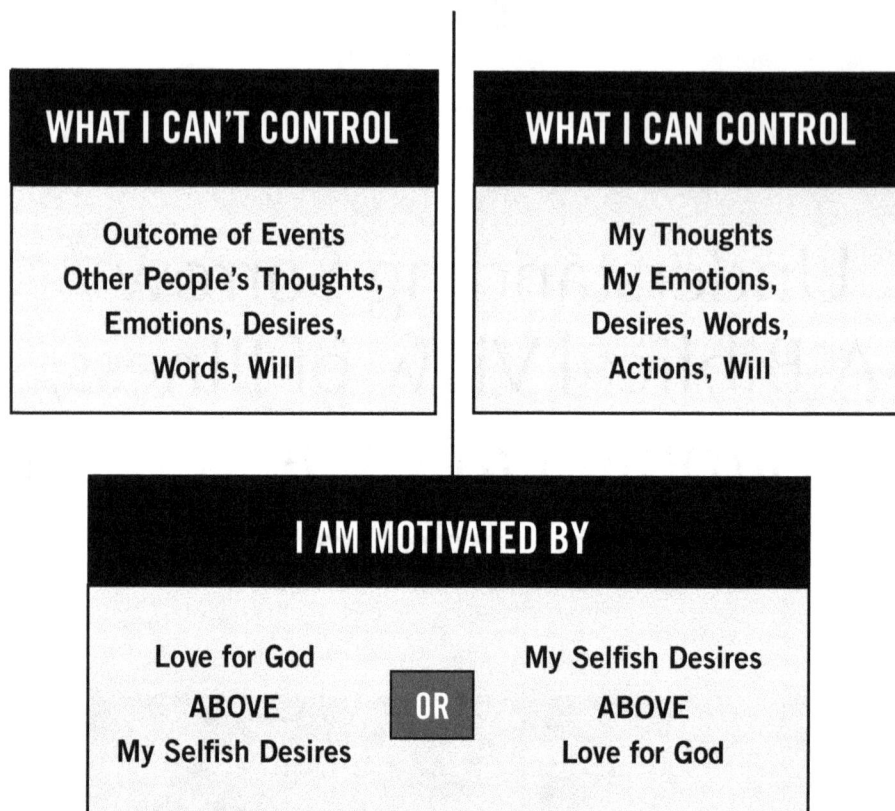

Understanding Sorrow

I. *Common* **Sorrow (Prov. 13:12, Job 1:13-22, 1 Peter 2:19, John 11:30-35, Rom. 12:15)**—a sadness of the soul due to a person's experiencing the disappointments of life, the difficulties of life, or the death of a loved one. For example, people can have a sadness of heart, yet without corresponding sin, as a result of:

A. Unmet expectations.

B. Experiencing tragedy in their lives or being mistreated by others.

C. Experiencing the death of someone they were attached to.

Response: We are to embrace the sovereignty, wisdom, and love of God in this sorrow as we walk through it. The goal is not to hinder or stop this sorrow, but to accept that God has our best interests at heart and will use it to His glory and our good overall.

II. *Chosen* **Sorrow (Ex. 16:7-8, Num. 14:1-2)**—a sadness of the soul created by a person's grumbling or complaining about her or his circumstances. For example, people do not like and are unwilling to accept:

A. What God has allowed in the circumstances, so they complain about it.

B. That other people are not operating as they would like them to, so they complain about it.

C. The difficulties in life, so they complain about it.

Response: We are to repent of our unloving attitudes and actions and embrace the sovereignty, wisdom, and love of God. We are to accept what God has allowed while submitting to what He has commanded.

III. *Conscience* **Sorrow (Rom. 2:14-15, 1 Sam. 24:1-5, 2 Sam. 24:10)**—a sadness of the soul as a result of a person's conscience bringing about feelings of guilt due to some act(s) of sin in her or his life. For example, a person's guilty conscience and sadness of soul can result from:

A. Thinking in a sinful manner.

B. Talking in a sinful manner.

C. Living in a sinful manner.

Response: We are to repent of our unloving attitudes and actions and embrace the sovereignty, wisdom, and love of God. We are to accept what God has allowed while submitting to what He has commanded.

IV. *Casualty* **Sorrow (Gen. 4:1-14, 2 Cor. 7:10)**—a sadness of the soul as a result of regret over the consequences of sinful choices, ultimately leading a person to death because of a lack of repentance. For example:

A. A person is sorrowful about what is going to happen to him or her as a result of the sin.

B. A person is not focused on how his or her sin has dishonored God or damaged others.

C. Since there is no change of heart but only grief about the issue, the person experiences more complications, problems, pain, and ultimately death because of the consequences of a continued life of sin.

Response: We are to repent of our unloving attitudes and actions and embrace the sovereignty, wisdom, and love of God. We are to accept what God has allowed while submitting to what He has commanded.

V. *Contrite* Sorrow (2 Cor. 7:10-11, Luke 18:9-14)—a sadness of the soul because a person is broken over her or his sin against God. For example:

A. A person is grieved over how his or her sin has dishonored God.

B. A person is grieved over how she or he has brought sorrow to God because of her or his sin.

C. As a result of grief over sin against God, the person wants and moves toward making things right with God according to God's will and ways.

Response: We are to repent of our unloving attitudes and actions and embrace the sovereignty, wisdom, and love of God. We are to accept what God has allowed while submitting to what He has commanded.

VI. *Chastisement* Sorrow (Heb. 12:11)—a sadness of soul because a person is experiencing the discipline of God that leads to a product of righteousness in their living. For example, people can be grieved as they experience the discipline of God:

A. That produces righteousness in their thoughts, desires, and motives.

B. That produces righteousness in their communication, behavior, manner of life, or manner of serving.

C. That produces righteousness in their relationship patterns.

Response: We are to endure the pain, accepting what God is allowing while submitting to what He has commanded.

Essential Practices to Consider Regarding Sorrow

I. Grieve the disappointment, death, difficulties, devastation, denial, damage, or distance that has happened.

II. Accept what God has allowed and surrender to the reality of God's will within the context of the sorrow.

III. Confess and repent of any and all unloving thoughts, desires, words, or actions.

IV. Identify, in light of your sorrow, the attribute of God most needed for you to depend on and embrace it by faith.

V. Adjust your desires to fit the situation and accept what you cannot have and have lost in the situation, while embracing what you can have and can continue to glean and gain from the situation.

VI. Identify the specific commands of Scripture that apply to your situation and seek to apply them.

Key Point: God uses sorrow in our lives. God controls the sorrow in our lives. We must trust God's love and learn how to handle sorrow accordingly. If we so choose, we can rely upon self and false hopes and be crushed in our spirit as a result when handling sorrow. Or we can choose to depend on God to go through and grow through our sorrow, resulting in a heart of gladness. For Christians, sorrow is never separated from the realities of our character deficiencies and the need to develop in Christ-like character and fellowship with God through the sorrow. How people respond to sorrow depends upon their relationship to God, their treasures, their hopes, their view of human nature, and in whom and in what they place their identities (Berger, *Rethinking Depression,* 121-27).

A Biblical View and Response to Physical Illness and Christians on Psychotropic Drugs

I. A Biblical View of Physical Illness

A. Illness exists because of the fall of Adam, which resulted in the curse of sin on our lives, leading to weak and frail bodies (Rom. 5:12, 1 Peter 1:24).

B. Illness may occur due to unconfessed sin in a person's life (Ps. 32:1-4).

C. Illness may occur because God is punishing an unbeliever (Ex. 15:26).

D. Illness may occur because God is disciplining a believer (2 Sam. 12:14-15).

E. Illness may occur because God is seeking to bring about repentance (1 Cor. 5:5).

F. Illness may occur because God is using it to prevent a person from sinning (2 Cor. 12:7).

G. Illness may occur as a natural consequence of a person's not taking care of his or her body (Prov. 19:16).

H. Illness may occur as a result of unbiblical thinking and actions (2 Chron. 26:19).

I. Illness can be used by God to bring glory to Himself (John 11:1-4).

J. Illness can be used by God to expose the character of a person (Job 2:1-6).

II. Key Perspectives for a Person to Consider When Struggling with a Physical Illness

A. There must be biblical understanding of physical illness (Rom. 12:2).

B. God has the physical illness under His sovereign control (Eccles. 7:13-14).

C. God will not allow physical illness to rise above what a Christian can handle (1 Cor, 10:13).

D. God will give what is needed so a person can function as God has commanded in spite of the physical sickness (2 Cor. 9:8).

E. God wants a person to be victorious, not a victim in response to physical sickness (1 Cor. 15:57, Job 1:1-2:10).

III. An Approach to Help People with Physical Illness through the Counseling Process

    A. Help the person to see God's perspective on illness.

    B. Help the person to focus more on becoming like Christ as the primary goal and getting over the illness by taking medicine or other methods as the secondary goal.

    C. Teach the person how use God's grace to function responsibly even when feeling horrible.

    D. Teach the person how to be thankful even when feeling terrible.

    E. Teach the person to focus on victory above relief.

    F. Remind the person to graciously give others in the church the blessing of opportunities to serve her or him.

IV. Distinguishing between the Material and Immaterial (Nonphysical) Aspects of Humans

Key Point: God's Word reveals that people's inner mental soundness is directly connected to those things for which they are responsible to God in their immaterial (nonphysical) being, not with those things for which they are not responsible. (Human wisdom blames the brain for that which the Bible holds the heart responsible.)

V. As created in the image of God, we are until death an inseparable unity of the material (body and brain) and the immaterial (heart or soul and spirit).

    A. We have been designed with a mind that involves our thoughts, beliefs, understanding, memory, judgment, imaginations, discernment, and conscience (Prov. 23:7; Rom. 12:2-3, 2:15-16; Mark 2:6; 2 Cor. 10:5).

    B. We have been designed with affections that involve our longings, desires, and feelings (Ps. 20:4; Eccles. 7:9, 11:9; Ps. 73:7; Jas. 3:14; Heb. 12:3; Joshua 14:8).

C. We have been designed with a will that involves our ability to choose and determine action (Deut. 30:19, Joshua 24:15, Ps. 25:12, Eccles. 2:4-8).

D. Our mind, affections, and will compose what we call the immaterial (non-physical) part of humans. The Bible generally uses the words *soul*, *spirit*, and *heart* when speaking of the immaterial aspect of a person (1 Cor. 2:11, Rom. 8:16, Prov. 4:23). Sometimes the word *soul* is used to describe the whole person, both material and immaterial (Acts 2:41).

E. We have been designed with a physical body, which is the home of the immaterial part of us (2 Cor. 5:1-10; Phil.1:19-23; 1 Cor. 9:27, 15:35-58).

F. The physical body and immaterial parts of a person are an inseparable union while that person is alive on earth (Gen. 2:7, 1 Cor. 15:35-38, Phil. 1:19-23).

G. We have each been created as an eternal being that will live forever either in fellowship with God or in eternal damnation (Luke 16:19-31, John 3:36, Rev. 20:11-15).

H. We are accountable to God for our thoughts, words, and deeds (2 Cor. 5:10, Rom. 14:10-12, Eccles. 12:13-14).

I. There is a distinction between the heart (soul and spirit) and the body; the heart (soul and spirit) is the real you and the body is the house in which the real you lives (Gen. 1:26, 2 Cor. 5:6-10, Phil. 1:19-23).

VI. Inside each of us, our immaterial heart is our individual personality, which is not confined to our material body and brain. Our individual personality keeps on living even after we die (Rev. 6:9-11; 1 Sam. 28:15-19; Luke 16:23-31, 9:28-31).

VII. Human Personality

Read these Scriptures: Revelation 6:9-11, Luke 9:28-31. Then analyze them and make a list below of characteristics that are usually associated with a person's brain but that in these instances are exhibited by people who are physically dead and have only their immaterial beings to account for the characteristics.

A. _____

B. _____

C. _____

D. _____

E. _____

F. _____

G. _____

H. _____

I. _____

J. _____

K. _____

L. _____

M. _____

N. _____

O. _____

Key Point: We find that many of those characteristics we assume are limited to the brain are not. A person's immaterial heart interfaces with his or her material brain while he or she functions on earth. After death many functions we associate with the brain continue in operation in a person's immaterial being. The heart chooses and the brain is involved, but it is the heart that drives the choices and not the brain. Our immaterial heart is the control center of those things for which we are responsible to God. Inside our immaterial heart is our individual personality, which is not confined to our material body and brain. Our individual personality keeps on living even after we die (Rev. 6:9-11, 1 Sam. 28:15-19, Luke 9:28-31).

VIII. A person's immaterial heart interfaces with her material brain in the area of thought. We need both the immaterial heart and material brain for the thought processes to happen while we are living. When we die, our thought processes continue in the immaterial heart.

A. Daniel 2:28 (He was thinking thoughts in his material brain.)

B. Daniel 2:30 (He was thinking thoughts in his immaterial heart.)

C. Song of Solomon 5:2 (Her heart was awake while her brain was unconscious.)

IX. Our material body and brain may limit or expand our ability to think or experience things here on earth, but the body and brain do not determine the thoughts, words, or actions for which we are responsible before God to choose in our immaterial heart. Some of us have great intellect, small intellect, or even an intellectual disability, but these issues do not affect the processes of the immaterial heart. Sin is not caused by the brain or brain chemicals but by the thought processes of the immaterial heart. Therefore, for a sin issue in our lives, we must blame the immaterial heart and not the material body and brain. Medicine may deal with the symptoms of the problem but not root issues (Matt. 15:17-20, Mark 7:18-23, Prov. 4:23, Phil. 4:8, Gal. 5:19-23, Prov. 18:14, 1 Cor. 10:13).

I have appreciated Rich Thomson's insights on the above topic in his book *The Heart of Man and the Mental Disorders*.

X. Points to Consider about Christians on Psychotropic Drugs [psycho (mind) + tropic (affecting) = mind altering/affecting drugs]

A. Christians who are on psychotropic drugs may be focused more on feeling better through the medication than becoming better through the biblical process of change.

B. Christians who use psychotropic drugs may not understand how to use the Bible to find God's solution to life's problems; therefore they are left to secular understanding about their problems, resulting in turning to psychotropic drugs as the solution.

C. Christians who use psychotropic drugs may be treated by professionals who deal only in psychotropic drugs to address the particular issues at hand.

D. Christians who use psychotropic drugs may believe that they cannot obey God when they feel bad; therefore they may believe that the only time they can be responsible is when they feel good by the use of medication.

E. Christians who use psychotropic drugs may have been told that their problems are based on physical conditions of the body that require medication.

F. Christians who use psychotropic drugs may not trust in the sufficiency of Scripture to handle their problems.

G. Christians who use psychotropic drugs may not understand or accept why and how God uses pain and trials to build character.

XI. Biblical Perspectives to Consider about Christians and Psychotropic Drugs

A. The Bible is sufficient to provide everything we need for life and godliness, which includes the bad feelings that people try to address through psychotropic drugs instead of the Messiah and His Word (2 Peter 1:1-11, 2 Tim. 3:16-17).

B. God's goal for our lives is not that we live to feel better but that we live to become better through the biblical process of change (Eph. 4:17-32, Col. 3:1-17).

C. When there is no organic basis found for discomfort or pain, you will find that unbiblical responses to life's situations are the core reasons for the discomfort/pain; therefore a psychotropic drug may deal with the pain or discomfort but it does not deal with the source of the discomfort (unbiblical responses) (Gen. 4:1-7, Rom. 2:14-15).

D. Sinful behavior and the bad feelings that follow do not come from organic problems of the body; sinful behavior comes from the wickedness of the heart. The bad feelings that follow come from the conscience that stimulates the sense of guilt, apparently uncaused fear, and the desire to flee when no one is chasing. Therefore psychotropic drugs are not the cure; the Messiah and His Word are the cure (Matt. 15:11-20, Mark 7:20-23, 2 Cor. 5:11-17).

E. Psychotropic drugs can make us *feel* better but they will not help us to *become* better (Gal. 5:16-19-26, Gen. 4:1-7, Rom. 7:4-8:15).

F. Medication is a great support but a terrible solution to nonorganic problems (Prov. 31:4-7).

XII. An Approach to Help Christians on Psychotropic Drugs

A. Help counselees identify the specific situations and problems that were happening to them, around them, or through them that led to taking psychotropic drugs.

B. Help counselees identify their responses and reactions in correlation to the specific situations and problems that led to taking psychotropic drugs.

C. Help counselees to identify the negative feelings that arose and how they chose to handle those negative feelings in correlation to the specific situations and problems.

D. Help counselees to identify their goals in the specific situations and problems (whether biblical or self-serving).

E. Help counselees identify their goals for taking psychotropic drugs in the specific situations and problems.

F. Help counselees to interpret life through biblical categories in correlation to their specific situations and problems.

G. Help counselees to apply biblical principles to the specific situations and problems so that they will focus more on being like Christ instead of merely feeling better in the crisis.

H. Help counselees to focus on becoming a better person through application of biblical principles to the specific situations and problems instead of feeling better in the specific situations and problems.

I. Coming off the medication is not the goal but rather helping the person to handle the specific situations and problems biblically.

J. As counselees come to see that they can handle the specific situations and problems through the power of God and the principles of His Word, whether they feel bad or not, they will begin to work on coming off the medication as a secondary goal as you have helped them to develop in the primary goal of becoming like Christ and handling situations biblically as they walk through life for God and others.

Key Point: Illness is a by-product of the curse of sin from the fall of Adam and the result of sin in one's life, yet God can use it for His glory and our good. When you have an illness there is something wrong in the tissues of your body, which can be proven by objective tests. Mental illness is really not an illness but truly an issue of the immaterial heart that needs to be addressed through the person of Jesus Christ, His power, and the principles of His Word. There may be physical issues that result from the spiritual problem that may require medication, but the root issue cannot be cured through medication but only through submission to the person and power of Jesus Christ.

In developing the above information, I have appreciated *The Christian Counselor's Medical Desk Reference* by Robert D. Smith, MD.

Source of Pain

Solution
Messiah
(Ps. 32:1-5)

Immaterial Aspects of Man
Or
Material Aspects of Man

Solution
Medication
(1 Tim. 5:23)

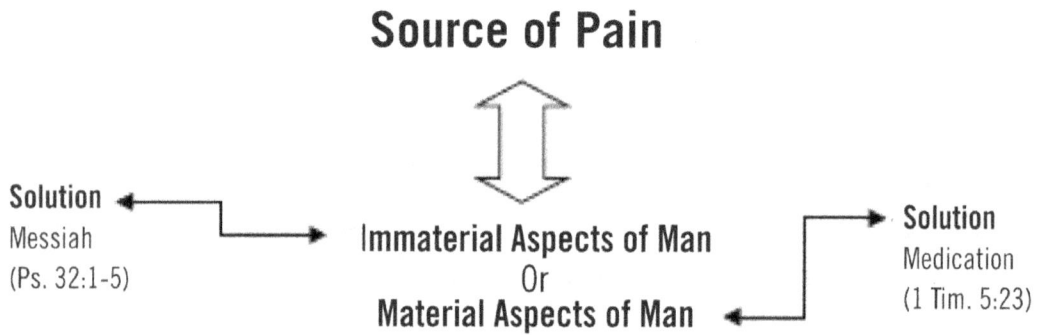

False Belief about Medication and Obedience

Pain < Obedience (Lesser the pain / greater my obedience)

Pain > Obedience (Greater the pain / lesser my obedience)

Therefore, medication is necessary for me to obey God.

False Conclusion: Medication brings relief of pain, resulting in a person's feeling better and being able to obey because of feeling better due to the medication.

Fallacy: A person believes that the power to obey is caused by feeling better as the result of taking the medication.

Truth: The power to obey is determined by the Holy Spirit, not by feeling better as a result of taking medication. Pain or lack of pain does not determine obedience (Rom. 8:1-15, Gal. 5:16-25).

Bibliography

Adams, Jay E. *The Christian Counselor's Manual: The Practice of Nouthetic Counseling*. The Jay Adams Library. Grand Rapids, MI: Zondervan, 1973.

———. *From Forgiven to Forgiving: Learning to Forgive One Another God's Way*. Amityville, NY: Calvary Press, 1994.

———. *How to Help People Change*. Grand Rapids, MI: Zondervan, 1986.

———. *Proverbs, The Christian Counselor's Commentary*. Cordova, TN: Institute for Nouthetic Studies, 2020.

Berg, Jim. *When Trouble Comes*. Greenville, SC: Bob Jones University Press, 2002.

Berger, Daniel R., II. *Rethinking Depression: Not a Sickness Not a Sin*. Taylors, SC: Alethia International Publications, 2019.

Boyer, James L. *For a World Like Ours: Studies in 1 Corinthians*. Grand Rapids, MI: Baker Book House, 1971.

Burroughs, Jeremiah. *The Rare Jewel of Christian Contentment*. 1648. Reprint, Carlisle, PA: The Banner of Truth Trust, 2002.

Cloud, Henry, and John Townsend. *Safe People*. Grand Rapids, MI: Zondervan Publishing House, 1995.

Dyer, Charles H. *Jeremiah*. In *The Bible Knowledge Commentary: An Exposition of the Scriptures*, edited by J.F. Walvoord and R.B. Zuck, 1:1132. Wheaton, IL: Victor Books, 1985.

Friesen, Garry. *Decision Making and the Will of God: A Biblical Alternative to the Traditional View*. Colorado Springs: Multnomah, 2004.

Holzmann, John. *Dating with Integrity*. Nashville: Word Publishing, 1992.

Keil, Carl Friedrich, and Franz Delitzsch. *Commentary on the Old Testament*, 6:213–14. Peabody, MA: Hendrickson, 1996.

Lane, Timothy S., and Paul David Tripp. *Relationships: A Mess Worth Making*. Greensboro, NC: New Growth Press, 2008.

MacArthur, John. *Counseling: How to Counsel Biblically*. Nashville: Thomas Nelson Publishers, 2005.

Scott, Stuart. *The Exemplary Husband*. Bemidji, MN: Focus Publishing Inc., 2000.

———. "Policies and Procedures Course." The Master's College (now The Master's University). Santa Clarita, CA: Graduate Program of Biblical Counseling, 2000.

Smith, Robert, D. *The Christian Counselor's Medical Desk Reference*. Woodruff, SC: Timeless Texts, 2004.

Thomson, Rich. *The Heart of Man and the Mental Disorders: How the Word of God Is Sufficient*. 2nd expanded ed. Alief, TX: Biblical Counseling Ministries, 2012.

Tripp, Paul David. *Instruments in the Redeemer's Hands: People in Need of Change Helping People in Need of Change*. Phillipsburg, NJ: P&R Publishing, 2002.

Viars, Steve. "Why Do We Need People" Sermon. Montgomery, AL: NANC Conference, 2003.

Welch, Ed T. *When People Are Big and God Is Small: Overcoming Peer Pressure, Co-dependency, and the Fear of Man*. Phillipsburg, NJ: P&R Publishing, 1997.

Helpful Resources Without Available Bibliographic Information

Dutton, Mark. "Idols of the Heart." Counseling Video Series. Faith Baptist Church, Lafayette, IN.

Macdonald, James. "No More People Pleasing." Sermon.

Scott, Stuart. *From Pride to Humility*. Booklet.

Shannon, Bill. "Till Death Do Us Part: A Biblical Look at Divorce and Remarriage." Teaching notes from Children's Ministry at Grace Community Church, Sun Valley, CA.

www.ingramcontent.com/pod-product-compliance
Lightning Source LLC
Chambersburg PA
CBHW081347280326
41927CB00042B/3217